Reconnecting, Redirecting, and Redefining 21st Century Males

Reconnecting, Redirecting, and Redefining 21st Century Males

H.E. "Doc" Holliday, PhD

ROWMAN & LITTLEFIELD EDUCATION

A division of

ROWMAN & LITTLEFIELD PUBLISHERS, INC.
Lanham • New York • Toronto • Plymouth, UK

Published by Rowman & Littlefield Education
A division of Rowman & Littlefield Publishers, Inc.
A wholly owned subsidary of The Rowman & Littlefield Publishing Group, Inc.
4501 Forbes Boulevard, Suite 200, Lanham, Maryland 20706
http://www.rowmaneducation.com

Estover Road, Plymouth PL6 7PY, United Kingdom

British Library Cataloguing in Publication Information Available

Library of Congress Cataloging-in-Publication Data

Holliday, H. E., 1948–
  Reconnecting, redirecting, and redefining 21st century males/H. E. "Doc" Holliday.
    p. cm.
  Includes bibliographical references and index.
  ISBN 978-1-61048-475-6 (cloth : alk. paper) — ISBN 978-1-61048-476-3 (pbk. : alk. paper) — ISBN 978-1-61048-477-0 (electronic)
  1. Boys. 2. Boys—Psychology. 3. Boys—Conduct of life. 4. Child development. 5. Men. I. Title.
  HQ775.H47 2011
  305.23081—dc23

                                                          2011016668

♾™ The paper used in this publication meets the minimum requirements of American National Standard for Information Sciences—Permanence of Paper for Printed Library Materials, ANSI/NISO Z39.48-1992.

Printed in the United States of America

Contents

Additional Praise   vii

Foreword   ix

Acknowledgments   xi

Introduction   xiii

Chapter 1   Defining the 21st Century Male   1

Chapter 2   Rebranding the 21st Century Male   31

Chapter 3   Mentoring and other Male Affiliations   51

Chapter 4   Families   69

Chapter 5   Parenting 21st Century Males   77

Chapter 6   Public Schools Evolving from Teachers to Academic Coaches   87

Chapter 7   Importance of Understanding   123

Chapter 8   Creating a Personal Vision   131

Chapter 9   Get off the Sidelines and into the Game   137

Chapter 10   Huddle-Up   145

References   163

Index   167

About the Author   171

Additional Praise

"This book offers sage advice for concerned citizens to ponder as we grapple with the complex problems that seem to be consuming far too many of our America's males. The dilemma can no longer be seen as an urban youth problem. The negative consequences are now pervasive in rural, suburban as well as in large cities. Caring adults must develop a more robust, relevant dialogue with our young men as a way to reconnect and to establish a new level of trust that will allow us to assist them in navigating the seemingly endless 21st century challenges they now encounter. This book outlines the many academic, physical, emotional, and psychological transitions boys are expected to navigate on their own. Dr. Holliday offers bold new strategies designed to capture the imagination of our youth and to encourage society in general to take a far different approach when engaging and interacting with young men."

—Dr. Daniel Papp, president, Kennesaw State University, Kennesaw, Georgia

"This book is a culmination of the numerous years Dr. H. E. "Doc" Holliday has spent trying to make a difference in the lives of our youth. He has put into print his insights that are a wealth of knowledge highlighting the problems, and remedies that can be used to offset the continued destruction of our youth, especially our black males. Making a difference in the lives of young black males has always been high on his list of priorities. In addition, Dr. Holliday has listed and recommended strategies that can be employed to mitigate this serious problem faced by young black males. Gender based education, school uniforms, mentoring, and leadership seminars are successful strategies Dr. Holliday has utilized as a building principal and central level office administrator.

"Dr. Holliday has utilized researched based data and the insights of highly respected practitioners, such as authors, consultants, and motivational speakers to support his assertions. I highly recommend this book be included in your arsenal as you attempt to become a change agent in the lives of young men and women."

—U.S. Davidson, Ph.D., Georgia Public School Administrator

"'Boys need structure. Boys need to be a part of a group.' As my son approached his teenage years, these words from Doc Holliday became a clear and true sentiment of my life. It is well understood that children should be well rounded. Often, we place them in activities to develop their talents and enhance their socialization. However, as a well educated single mom it escaped me how important these activities are in addressing the unique challenges I faced with my son as he struggled to attain academic success while balancing his emerging social interest. This is an engaging conversation on overcoming the challenges that arises at various stages in the lives of our sons. The book helped to place a number of things into perspective regarding raising a male child successfully. While the book addresses some inadequacy in the education system, the main premise of the text is to get to the heart of what is needed to educate the black male. Doc Holliday conducted extensive research to provide timely insight on how to affirm our sons' identity and how to reinforce the importance of education. The book is a must read for parents seeking practical methods and insight that will minimize the isolation often encountered by African-American males in the education system."

—Leyte Winfield, Ph.D., associate professor of organic chemistry,
Spelman College, Atlanta, Georgia

Foreword

Dr. H. E. Holliday's book is a must read for creating a positive shift in the direction and mindset of young boys. Why are we losing so many young boys? Why are they losing interest in school? Why have they lost the motivation to dream big and excel in the classroom and in life? Dr. Holliday's book will help you see the contributing factors to these trends. There are many factors that contribute to this mindset and trend. After exploring the factors this book is a solution based resource book that will open the reader's eyes to see how we can redirect our young boys into a positive direction.

Dr. Holliday has spent numerous hours researching why we are losing so many males as they navigate through life from being boys to becoming men. Not only has Dr. Holliday researched the subject but he has applied his research, strategies and principles while holding top positions in the field of education. He has held the position of Principal, Assistant Superintendent and Chief of Staff just to name a few titles. As an educator, Dr. Holliday would always research the data at each school where he worked in the past and he would develop programs that would increase academic achievement based on the data. Dr. Holliday realized that education is not a one size fits all. He developed programs for boys and girls that would target their needs.

Dr. Holliday's book will provide readers with proven tools, strategies, and principles that will help young boys become successful young men. This book removes the guesswork. It will give you a blueprint backed with proven strategies. If we want to change things, we must change what we are doing. The problem is how we see the problem. Dr. Holliday has identified the problem but provided solutions that can be applied to give young boys the tools needed to become successful young men. Dr. Holliday has identified some "core values" that young boys must learn and embrace in order to attain any level of success. This book is a must read if we are going to reclaim our young boys.

—Mike Howard, Motivational Speaker

Acknowledgments

I especially thank Mary Louise Frazier and my wife Sarah Nell Holliday for their tireless work editing this book. I appreciate the long hours and care you provided in helping to reshape this important message.

Every 21st Century Boy and Girl in America Deserves a Luther in Their Lives.

Luther Henry Holliday, my father, meant the world to me and my brothers and sisters. He was a "Southern Boy" from rural Georgia who moved North in the 1940s to pursue a better life for his wife (Ruby Zachery). Now, Luther was a big gregarious man who already had a personal vision and family goals once he arrived in Ohio. He believed that hard work and determination combined with attaining a quality education would not only level the playing field but provide a bright future for his wife and children. Luther never earned a four year college degree but he had a Ph.D. in common sense and relationship building. He was a demanding, but, nurturing father who only accepted your very best efforts. He never asked for a handout. He was like the old James Brown song "You don't have to give me nothing . . . just open up the door and I will get it myself."

He instilled in all who made contact with him the belief that "you can achieve anything in life that you want if you set your mind to it." This was the advice from a man who absolutely believed in self discipline of mind, body, and soul. He did not allow us to take the easy way out, to quit, or to make excuses. One of the best qualities of Luther was his willingness to help others. He was well regarded by his family, friends, church, work associates and his community. My father was once banned from sitting on his front porch by several of his neighbors. If you are wondering why such an affable man would be disliked by so many people who lived around him . . . let me explain. It seems as though that even the mailmen liked to spend time around Luther. As a matter of fact there were many days while making mail deliveries to our home . . . the mailman would take it upon himself to sit on our front porch and spend an extra 20–30 minutes talking to Luther. It appears that something or someone could actually delay mail delivery in the United States . . . and his name was Luther. One can not help but reminisce and cherish the many lessons in life that Luther Henry Holliday taught his children (Louise, Earl, Jerry, Tony, Chris and Sheryl) and grandchildren. There were countless other individuals that had the pleasure of knowing and loving him. Hence, it is my sincere belief that each boy and girl in American deserves a Luther in their lives.

Thank you Daddy!

Introduction

America's public schools are undergoing gut wrenching, fundamental changes as we move further into the 21st century. The growing dropout problem, the downward trend in standardized test scores, and the dramatic increase in violence leads one to believe that far too many of today's boys have lost hope and are simply out of control. One of American public schools' greatest challenges is the startling decline in academic performance by public school boys.

How does one explain award winning athletic teams in the same school that houses chronically dangerous classrooms that lead to wretchedly lower standardized test scores? Whatever happened to the concept of Scholar Athletes? Why do boys now feel that they can only become one at the exclusion of the other? Why has the relationship between our primarily female teaching staff and our boys become so toxic and adversarial? How have new societal norms and expectations contributed to this growing phenomenon, and more importantly, what can be done to construct a new, vastly improved model? This is not rocket science! We must, in many cases, go back to the basics! Many of the most successful solutions have much to do with common sense, relationship building, and a commitment and willingness to share our time, talents, and wisdom with others.

This book will address a growing dilemma experienced by many 21st century school aged males. It will identify many of the academic, physical, emotional, and psychological transitions of boys from their earliest stages of development to the next. Why don't more of our boys understand that they must personally navigate these stages in order to achieve individual success as they evolve in life? One theory centers on the absence of verbal instructions and historical expectations that men once passed down from generation to generation through oral traditions, language, and community interactions.

In recent years this once typically reliable oral supply line has been inalterably interrupted. There is now a preponderance of single women raising sons in an increasingly complex, mobile United States.

It is little wonder that a record number of boys are opting out of the "Old School" traditional roles that were once an integral part of America's culture less than a generation ago. It is not so much that boys are not interested in being successful in whatever field they choose in today's frenetic world as it is about knowing how to win in the game of "Life". We must begin to teach these young men "How to Play the Game". We must begin to inspire our young men to believe and understand that life is much richer when you have options. It is apparent that this dramatic, yet simple, message is not being passed on to a growing number of young men especially in their most formative years.

This book will examine some the transitions that most 21st century boys are making in isolation and how we must reverse their belief that no one really understands or cares about them. This book will share research about the state of boys in America and how we must go about the task of assisting them in rebranding themselves. This book will discuss and shed light on the new 21st century value system that encourages many boys from engaging in activities that are self destructive, anti intellectual, and too often misogynous rhetoric.

This book will illustrate why "Belief and Trust" are critically important if we are to draw many of these young men back into mainstream America. This book will review new cutting edge ideas that adults must familiarize themselves with if we are to reposition America's public schools to one of relevance and to once again become the model system for the world to emulate. This book will examine the power of "Sports Metaphors" and outline how they can become a bridge between the growing communications gap between adults and 21st century males.

Over the years, this author has been a father, family elder, mentor, confidant building principal, and resident sage to thousands of young men of all ages and races. One must always lead by example and be a discerning listener before ever attempting to help individuals develop a personal plan of action. Stephen Covey said it best when he strongly intimated "that we should first seek to understand and then to be understood". That, more than anything, will enabled adults to reconnect with young people of all walks of life.

We should always hearken back to the time that we walked in their shoes. One must never be too judgmental, just be someone who truly pays close attention to their heartfelt and very personal thoughts. Each chapter begins with excerpts from a song with a message. Each song's lyrics are meant to resonate with oral clues pertaining to each specific chapter. This is another way of bridging the 20th Century era with a melancholy yet, potent piece of advice for 21st Century males.

Chapter 1

Defining the 21st Century Male

Songwriter Marvin Gaye's 1971, hit song "Mercy, Mercy Me" did a masterful job of summing up the woeful attitude and state of affairs of far too many of the best and brightest young men in America at that time! There was a sense of hopelessness and despair that permeated the land. Unfortunately, things have not dramatically improved over the past forty years. Throughout this book this author will define boys as males between the ages of four and twelve and young men as males between the ages of thirteen and twenty one.

What is physically and psychologically happening to young men all over the United States needs to be discussed in detail. This is no longer a problem solely in our inner cities. We need to explore and identify the new value and belief systems of our young men to better understand how it has negatively impacted our public schools and individual communities. It is our responsibility to find out as much about our sons, grandsons, nephews, neighbors, athletes, and students before we can ever begin to assist them with their transitions in life.

A transition is defined as the act of passing from one state or place to the next. The question which demands to be answered is why are so many of our young men failing to move from a healthy adolescent experience into the challenging teenage years and eventually into adulthood? The companion question should be what can adults do to make these essential transitions go as smoothly as possible? Why is it that many young men attending American public schools now see themselves as either scholars or athletes (jocks)?

Just a few short years ago we managed to combine both of these roles. This was considered the norm in most of America's public schools. This was thought of as a very realistic goal for many young men growing up in the

1960s, 1970s, and 1980s. We must once again unite the love of learning with life long lessons attained through athletic competition.

A new "Male Initiative" must be crafted, debated, and ultimately implemented that involves cutting edge ideas, strategies and changes. Caring adults can then begin to reconnect with this hugely disenchanted and detached segment of our country. Our success in developing relationships with these young men will ultimately impact the future of our nation. The United States can no longer continue to write off these large, growing segments of our population as chronically underperforming who are incapable of making valuable contributions to our society.

America's economy, safety, productivity and reputation as a world leader will depend on our success in resolving these unprecedented life challenges. We can no longer afford to look the other way and hope these issues dissipate or resolve themselves. There is now a sense of urgency that demands that we address these concerns with all due dispatch! We must summon up our collective wisdom to put into place solutions that will resonate with all 21st century children, especially young men.

Much has been written and discussed about the challenges of 21st century males in recent years. This book is meant to examine how parents, coaches, and educators develop these young minds as they transition onto their next phase of physiological and intellectual development. Several promising approaches and theories will be examined and discussed regarding this very sensitive subject. We need only to look at America's declining public schools, the expanding juvenile justice system or the exponential growth of female dominated single parent families to gain a glimpse of the extent of our nation's problems.

Can our elected and appointed leaders provide the wisdom and will to creatively address these concerns with substantive and meaningful programs? This author believes that America can and should take a grassroots approach when addressing the needs of our schools and communities. Each of us must assume a role and responsibility for creating healthy children. We must act now if we are to prepare young men to grow and prosper intellectually. We must not delay for risk of losing another generation of young talented men who will otherwise wonder aimlessly through life never reaching their true potential.

There has been a dramatic decline of interactions between generations over the past fifty years. This has lead to a catastrophic disruption of "Oral Traditions" that were once automatically shared between males for hundreds of years. These untold stories, expectations, and manly conversations were handed down from father to son, from grandfather to grandchildren, from uncles to nephews, from neighbor to neighbor, from elder statesmen to up and coming young men. This knowledge has been typically passed down from one generation to another in two primary ways. It is passed by speaking and also through writing. It is often taught without words by showing people how to do things.

Young people have often learned in the past by watching their elders perform specific duties. Oral tradition is interpreted as the passing of verbal knowledge from one generation to the next. Many traditions and expectations were preserved and continued to exist because they were passed down through these traditions until recently. Many unspoken ways of behaving and doing things were taught by telling and showing one another how to perform these tasks. Elders are very important in cultures that teach and rely on these oral traditions.

The elders are the experienced people with the most knowledge. They have gained this information over their lifetime and they are expected and needed to teach the younger generation. No culture remains completely unchanged. New knowledge is sometimes introduced and at times lost as that culture expands or contracts. Traditional knowledge is susceptible to change over time.

THE CRISIS OF LOSING TRADITIONAL KNOWLEDGE

The education of more and more of America's male children comes from the media and books rather than from trusted elders. Children need to go to school because there are new skills to learn about while navigating the new global society. They need to learn skills such as reading, writing, mathematics and relationship development as well as becoming proficient using technology. These efforts will lead toward securing jobs that will help one gain entry into the prized American middle class. Over time, less of this knowledge has come from the oral traditions within one's own culture.

The role of the elders of passing along valuable life lessons to young people has diminished at a rapid clip over the past fifty years. It is evident that elders do not have as important a role as they once had in passing along their wisdom to younger people. In many communities the children do not speak the language of their elders. There are those individuals who consider this an insignificant trade off in the name of modern day progress. This reduces the chances for elders to teach them. These changes mean that much valuable traditional knowledge is being lost. The increase in computer texting, slang, gestures, and hip hop music presents a new set of challenges when attempting to bridge the communications gap between younger and older males throughout the 21st century culture.

The knowledge that is being irretrievably lost could have provided young people with a sense of identity. This has generated a crisis on many fronts. The reduction of self worth and the loss of self esteem are identified as critical challenges facing many young men today. Experts agree that healthy individuals generally have a strong desire to know something about their past in order to develop a pride in their culture. Elders must have a greater role in passing on the knowledge that is important for survival. Elders know a lot about the norms and culture of America. Elders are knowledgeable about how to successfully play this game of life under almost any condition. This is why traditional knowledge still has many uses in our world today.

There are strikingly negative results when traditional knowledge is interrupted and left up to the interpretation of the younger generation. A good example in the animal kingdom that humans can draw a parallel to is what occurred in an African Animal Reserve where juvenile elephants were going on a killing rampage of rhinoceros for no apparent reasons. This is, of course unnatural behavior on the part of the elephant and it caused great disruption in an otherwise tranquil environment.

After careful study of this baffling problem it was theorized that the young juveniles in this particular game reserve had been abandoned early in life by their parents and consequently knew nothing about interacting with other species within their environment. They had created their own negative tradition of killing rhinoceros. The animal game officials decided to tackle this problem by introducing two experienced older male elephants to live with the juveniles and to model the type of expected behavior. The experienced males began to immediately create a more traditional positive interaction between elephants and rhinoceros. The killing by the juveniles came to an immediate halt and the two species began to peaceably coexist once again.

Another good example of this knowledge is the story regarding Socrates. Years ago a young man came to visit Socrates with the hope of learning everything that he could so that he could immediately be just as wise. Socrates accommodated the young man for many days until Socrates thought of an important test to give the young man. Socrates took the young man down to the beach and instructed him to get on his shoulders as they proceeded to walk out into the ocean. After going out far enough from shore that it posed a danger to the young man, Socrates dropped him from his shoulders and proceeded back onto the beach alone. The young man was not a very good swimmer and struggled and nearly died.

Upon reaching the shore, the young man swore vengeance on the life of Socrates. He found Socrates at his home quietly tending to his everyday life's chores. The young man screamed at him and asked him why he had abandoned him. Socrates, in a very calm voice asked the young man, when you were out in the water struggling to survive, what did you desire most? The young man was angry, but managed to compose himself and answered.

I wanted more than anything else to live. Socrates responded that if you desire as much to be wise as you did to live then you shall succeed! This story tells us much about the desires of our youth. They often want immediate benefits without paying the price for success. It generally takes time to put into position all of the wonderful things that one desires out of life. There are no shortcuts!

CORE VALUES WORTH KNOWING

There is a growing disconnect between the real world and the perceived world of 21st century boys. Many young men do not know what society expects of them as they struggle with securing their place in our increasingly complicated universe. They far too often embrace concepts that are either risky or lack substance. The following are Core Values that have withstood the test of time that every young man should become familiar with:

1. The importance of attaining a quality education.
2. The importance of family and true friends.
3. The importance of a strong work ethic.
4. The importance of treating women with respect and dignity.
5. The importance of delaying immediate gratification/begin to plan for the future.
6. The importance of respecting adults and authority.
7. The importance of having a strong personal spiritual base.
8. The importance of looking and acting like you are "About Something"
9. The importance of learning to work with both your hands and your mind.
10. The importance of networking in the "at large" community.
11. The importance of joining an organization or sports team (no man is an island).
12. The importance of maintaining your poise while under pressure.
13. The importance of saving for a rainy day.
14. The importance of always striving for excellence in everything that you do.
15. The importance of being physically fit.
16. The importance of pursuing self actualization (Maslow's Theory).
17. The importance of freeing your mind from hatred.
18. The importance of giving more than you receive and to always help others.

19. The importance of thinking with a positive outlook.
20. The importance of fearing/respecting someone or something.
21. The importance of setting personal goals.
22. The importance of being humble and to walk softly but, carry a big stick . . .
23. The importance of developing your personal man-tra/vision.
24. The importance of reading and listening between the lines.
25. The importance of moving from poverty thinking to middle class thinking.
26. The importance of being well read and informed.
27. The importance of being twice as good and twice as prepared as your competition.
28. The importance of developing self discipline.
29. The importance of understanding and embracing technology.
30. The importance of maintaining balance in your life.

HIERARCHY OF BASIC NEEDS

Abraham Maslow developed a theory of personality that has influenced a number of different fields, including education. This far reaching influence is due in part to the high level of practicality of Maslow's theory. This theory accurately describes many realities of personal experiences. Many people identify with and understand what Maslow said. They often recognize some features of their personal experience or behavior which they have never put into words.

Maslow set up a hierarchy theory of needs. All of the basic needs are the equivalent of instincts in animals. Humans start with a very weak composition that becomes fully developed as the person grows. If their personal environment is positive people will grow straight and beautiful, actualizing the potentials they have inherited. If their environment is negative, they will not grow tall and straight and upright.

Maslow set up a hierarchy of five levels of basic needs. Higher levels of needs exist beyond the basics. These include needs for understanding, esthetic appreciation and purely spiritual needs. In the levels of the five basic needs, the person does not feel the second need until the demands of the first have been satisfied, then the second and so on. Maslow's basic needs are as follows:

1. Physiological Needs: These are biological needs. They consist of needs for oxygen, food, water, and a relatively constant body temperature. They are the strongest needs because if a person were deprived of all needs, the physiological ones would come first in the person's search for satisfaction.

2. Safety Needs: When all physiological needs are satisfied and are no longer controlling thoughts and behaviors, the needs for security is essential. Adults have little awareness of their security needs except in times of emergency or periods of disorganization in the social structure. Children often display the signs of insecurity and the desire to be safe.
3. Needs of Love, Affection and Belongingness: When the needs for safety and for physiological well-being are satisfied, the next class of needs for love, affection and belongingness can emerge. Maslow states that people seek to overcome feelings of loneliness and alienation. This involves both giving and receiving love, affection and the sense of belonging.
4. Needs for Esteem: When the first three classes of needs are satisfied, the need for esteem becomes prominent. These involve needs for both self-esteem and for the esteem a person gets from others. Humans have a need for a stable, firmly based high level of self-respect, and respect from others. When these needs are satisfied, the person feels self-confident and valuable as a person in the world. When these needs are frustrated, the person feels inferior, weak, helpless and worthless.
5. Needs for Self-Actualization: When the first four needs are satisfied the needs for self-actualization is activated. Maslow describes self-actualization as a person's needs to be and do that which the person was born to do. A musician must make music, an artist must paint, an orator must speak, a doctor must operate, and a poet must write. These needs make themselves felt in signs of restlessness. The person feels on edge, tense, lacking something, in short, restless. If a person is hungry, unsafe, not loved or unaccepted, or lacking self-esteem, it is very easy to know what the person is restless about. It is not always clear what a person wants when there is a need for self-actualization.

This theory is often represented as a pyramid, with the larger, lower levels representing the lower needs, and the upper point representing the need for self-actualization. Maslow believed that the only reason that people would not move well in the direction of self-actualization is because of hurdles placed in their way by society. He stated that education is one of these challenges. He recommended ways that education should switch from its usual person-stunting tactics to person growing approaches. Maslow noted that educators should respond to the potential of an individual and should address the following concepts:

1. Education should teach students to be authentic, to be aware of their inner selves and to hear their inner-feeling voices.

2. Education should teach students to transcend their cultural conditioning and become world citizens.
3. Education should help students discover their vocation in life, their calling, fate or destiny. This is especially focused on finding the right career and the right mate.
4. Education should teach students that life is precious, that there is joy to be experienced in life, and if people are open to seeing the good and joy in all kinds of situations, it makes life worth living.
5. Education must accept the students as he or she is and helps the person learn their inner nature. From real knowledge of aptitudes and limitations we can know what to build upon, what potentials are really there?
6. Education must see that the student's basic needs are satisfied. This includes safety, belongingness, and esteem needs.
7. Education should readdress consciousness, teaching the student to appreciate beauty and the other good things in nature and in living.
8. Education should teach students that controls are good, and complete abandon is bad. It takes control to improve the quality of life in all areas.
9. Education should teach students to transcend the insignificant problems and grapple with the serious problems of life. These include the problems of injustice, of pain, suffering, and death.
10. Education must teach students to select wisely. They must be given practice in making good choices.

Unfortunately, far too many 21st century young men never get past the initial physiological and safety needs of Maslow's Hierarchy of Needs. These are the basic needs of food, water, and shelter. These needs determine whether or not individuals ever meet any personal degree of self satisfaction during each day. Maslow's second need is one of safety and it has unparalleled importance as young men navigate their ever increasingly violent environments. With young men so preoccupied with the most basic needs of safety and survival it no wonder that Maslow's other needs are rarely achieved in sufficient enough numbers.

Several years ago a bestselling book talked about the predictability of the life stages all adults must go through. An analogy noted that man was like a lobster that outgrows and continuously sheds old skins. Man has no choice in the matter. You either evolve or wither away! Each time that the lobster expanded from within, the confining shell must be cast aside. Humans like lobsters, are left exposed and unsure of themselves until their new protective shell is fully formed. Humans experience similar growth spurts that demand that we evolve from a more protective, personal, physical space to one that is often uncomfortable and less familiar.

Over the years the lobster makes the necessary adjustments and evolutions that allow it to reach adult maturity. Humans must similarly go through a series of iterations (infancy, primary years, teenager, and young adulthood) before settling into a relatively harmonious and tranquil mature adult period of time. Each of these human passages is expected to provide an even better external and internal adjustment than the last one. Each of these new passages, similar to the lobster, presents a new series of physical and emotionally challenges and makes one somewhat vulnerable until we successfully move to that next evolutionary level.

Humans are expected to negotiate each of these passages in life. Each passage is distinctly different from the preceding one and yet, without fail, we manage through ingenuity and instinct. Each time we shed one relative period of safety we almost immediately begin to negotiate the next phase. The same growth process begins all over again. Well adjusted humans understand that the current passage or stage of life that we are experiencing will not last forever. Humans also understand that there will be periods, just like the lobster, when it appears that we are fighting for our very own survival.

Mankind is continuously evaluating how it feels about its status and position in the world today. Does its environment offer safety and consistency or does it need radical changes before it can begin to make personal sense? Finally, one must decide how we feel about our current way of living because we will undergo subsequent changes in four primary areas. They are as follows:

1. How one feels about self in relation to others?
2. How safety impacts your current life?
3. How is time perceived? Does one have an abundance of it or not?
4. How one expects to live life, to its fullest or is life full of despair?

What's Different About 21st Century Boys?

Adults who are responsible for shaping the next generation of young men often ask the following question. What makes a young man act the way he does? What is it about a boy that compels him to tempt fate and always be the ultimate risk taker? Many boys are often overly competitive and eager to challenge the odds and resist what typical adults refer to as common sense approaches to addressing problems. The continuous presence of testosterone is difficult for most mature males to deal with and it is especially challenging for our young men.

The surge of testosterone accounts for this newfound manliness. This maleness is thought to be the cause of much of the grief that has surrounded the lives of out of controlled young men in America today! Testosterone will have a continuous impact on the lives of young men beginning with puberty until they become seasoned men.

This powerful chemical will be responsible for driving some of the illogical and wild impulses of males for the rest of their lives. The sometimes outrageous behavior of males can be incomprehensible to adults. Many parents are at a loss when attempting to explain their son's oftentimes nontraditional behavior. Some parents may feel a sense of hopelessness when attempting to rationalize their behavior but at the same time, they desire to better understand their boys. It is as though they are suddenly living with a stranger who seems to have rejected all of the common sense values (self discipline, respect for authority, strong work ethic) that parents have instilled in them during the first few years of their young lives.

Adults should not write off our children too soon! We must better understand what drives their behavior and remain patient with them. We must help them get through this very difficult period and not attempt to fix all of the illogical things they do. It is a transition that they must personally undergo that is a major component of the growth cycle of young men whether we like it or not!

25 YEARS OF STRUCTURAL CHANGES

Things have radically changed in America and across the world over the past 20–25 years. Some changes have been welcomed with open arms and yet others have been slow to be embraced by the masses. This has had disastrous results for those who refused to adapt in a timely manner. The following is a list of the most notable changes that have impacted our lives over the last half of the 20th century.

1. Automobiles have changed and continue to evolve from the old gas guzzler to the more efficient high mileage vehicles. Long gone are the days of cars with big tail fins and environmentally unfriendly SUVs. The soaring cost of gasoline has demanded that we dramatically reduce our dependency on our preference for riding solo. We must embrace mass transit and other fuel saving measures. It has forced us to make lifestyle changes in the way we live and take care of our environment. General Motors was once the standard bearer for American industrial might. That of course is no longer the case! We are now in the process of mass production of battery operated cars.

2. Our economy has radically changed from an agrarian, to a manufacturing and ultimately to knowledge based high technology environments where individual intellect is essential for any advancement. Not too long ago it

seemed that each small town had its own mill or factory which offered a safety net to those individuals who chose not to matriculate to the traditional two or four year colleges. Today's economy mandates that we evolve into life long learners who understand the need for continuous updating and retraining.

3. Computer Technology changes by the moment and the digital divide is as apparent as ever before between the 'Haves and the Have Not's. There is an ever growing chasm between the technology comfort levels of older citizens when compared with the younger generation. The relatively new concept of digital natives and digital immigrants has been explored in recent books and articles. Today's generation of young people grew up with MTV, text messaging, cell phones, and laptops. These new innovative breakthroughs will continue to expand at warp speed. It is incumbent that adults stay current and not leave generations of students behind because of their lack of exposure to new technological breakthroughs.

4. Churches have transformed from being the small center of our local communities into large mega congregations that sometimes seem to be more interested in generating money as opposed to saving and enriching the lives of its congregations. Many churches are no longer seen as places of refuge and spiritual healing. Far too many young men see church as out of step with the 21st century lifestyles they embrace. They often note that churches offer little connection and even less satisfaction to the challenges young men face in today's world. A mega church is defined as having between 4000–6000 members or more. The Online Church appears to be the most rapidly growing segment of religion in the 21st century.

5. The World Map has changed with the emergence of the dismantling of the former Russian empire. Remember the East and West Germany unification, African colonization, and other changes that have occurred during the later part of the 20th century. There has been a steady transition of people moving from the countryside to urban centers since the 1920s. This phenomenon has helped to disrupt the traditional family life where boys remained in close contact with extended family members for much longer periods of time. This ensured that most young men were connected to their nuclear family and were expected to act and behave in an acceptable manner.

6. Medicine has changed so dramatically that doctors can now diagnose sick patients by simply having them walk through the door of a wired examination room. We are no longer assigned a death warrant for cancer and many other medical scourges of the past such as polio, mumps,

typhoid fever, and internal medicines. We still have much research to resolve many vexing challenges such as AIDS but most experts agree that progress is being made.

7. The global economy of most nations is now inextricably linked at the hip with most other industrial countries. The economic emergence of burgeoning superpowers like China, India and Brazil are now forces to be reckoned with. The G20 Nations now cooperate when addressing worldwide economic issues. America can no longer act independently or only in its own self interest. The current economic recession is a worldwide event because of the interconnectedness of the world finances. Where we once were a solvent nation we are now considered a debtor nation who is held accountable to other world powers.

8. The Stock Market has moved from a relatively modest 3,000 to the recently achieved 13,000 (2008) milestone and has now dropped between 7,000–10,000 levels. The "Wall Street "meltdown and its subsequent impact on other world economies illustrate how the world now moves in unison in many instances. America can now experience wildly fluctuating stock market results in a matter of minutes and hours because of international monetary transactions beyond its borders.

9. The family composition has changed from the traditional form of man/ wife and 2.5 children to a blended one where there are many alternatives to the traditional old model. We now see more and more blended families, interracial, step, and gay families.

10. Public Schools have failed to make market adjustments fast enough during the later part of the 20th century. America has sacrificed quality in the quest to make schools more efficient. Big schools do not always equate to increased effectiveness. It has often been suggested that if an alien had visited a public school classroom in 1970, and revisited that same classroom again in 2010, that he would be hard pressed to find substantive difference in the delivery of education by classroom teachers. There will generally be an adult at the front of the room talking to children seated in nice little rows trying their best to passively follow along. There have been educational advances in parts of the United States but it is uneven and not consistent in far too many public schools.

Our public schools have evolved from K-12 systems that were highly respected and emulated around the world into organizations where large numbers of students are warehoused into numbingly listless silos conducted under extraordinarily anti intellectual conditions. Many American schools are no longer seen as cherished and valued experiences that challenge young minds to sharpen their academic skills. Far too many young men go to school for the wrong reasons (sports, girls, food, and socialization). Many middle class parents have all but abandoned any reasonable hope that public schools will provide a valuable experience for their children.

Public schools have failed to embrace up to date strategies that encourage our young men to use their intellectual talents. These are some of the reasons American public schools have averaged over 2 million dropouts per year since 2005 (US Department of Education statistics). Young and old Americans have had to wrestle with significant lifestyle changes and have managed to make accommodations and adjustments.

However, many of America's young men seem to be faring less well than the general population. It is as though many of our boys have lost their way! They have fallen and cannot pull themselves up. Our young men need America's wisest and brightest citizens to collectively come together to lend a helping hand to guide them back to a productive and healthy lifestyle where they can realize their true potential.

CHALLENGE OF BEING ALL ALONE

Many experts note that the challenges facing many young males begin long before they enter school and continue throughout their entire life. One of the most difficult relationships to unravel is the intergenerational effect of difficult childhoods, poverty, and father absence for growing numbers of males. Their time spent in school leaves many young men disinterested in learning and unprepared to successfully enter the workplace. A poor education translates into joblessness and a lower quality of life for any adult and especially young men. The social role of men was always to become family providers and caring fathers. It is now considered beyond the reach of many males who are ill prepared to successfully compete in the workplace.

The public's perception of the young American males as violent, conniving, disrespectful, and unintelligent is widespread among our population. These images not only carry over into schools, affecting how males are treated, but typically influence the perceptions of people within the "at large" community. Males appear in large numbers in most categories of academic failure such as suspensions, special education classes, grade retention, and academic failure. There is growing sentiment that this social reality is neither accidental nor a random occurrence. Much of the research on the schooling experiences of males has included case studies, and relatively small accounts that inform the public of the true scope of this problem.

We all know that we now live in a global society where we pride ourselves on our interconnectedness. America has over 300 million people and yet, many young men today feel that they live in isolation. Many of our schools are populated by thousands of students yet, boys complain more and more about being all alone. What impact does the role of isolation play in America's 21st century public schools? The question must be raised in spite of the fact that schools and student populations have grown exponentially during the last half of the 20th century.

The one-room schoolhouse has been replaced by multi leveled buildings, complex levels of certified teachers and staffs, along with multimillion dollar school budgets. How can students feel isolated in spite of school buildings that house hundreds and sometimes thousands of students and what impact does isolation have on boys?

Some experts believe that living in bustling environments yet still feeling lonely has more to do with the changing roles of men and women and the crisis of expectations. There are some who believe that the rise of the modern feminist movement significantly altered the expectations that men had of women and that women had of men. Some experts rationalized that loneliness comes in two varieties. The first is the loneliness felt by single, shy people who have no friends. The second involves the person in a relationship who nevertheless feels isolated and very much alone.

MALE LONELINESS

Social psychologists have a growing concern about the male who has no apparent friends. Many studies have concluded that women have better relationship skills which help them to be more successful at making and keeping friends. Women are more likely than men to express their emotions and display empathy and compassion in response to the emotions of others. Men are more isolated and competitive and therefore have fewer close friends. Some men may not even be conscious of their loneliness and isolation.

Some experts have researched the barriers that inhibit the development of friendships among men. They are as follows:

1. Males strongly resist showing any type of emotions. The adage big boys don't cry is especially true among young males today. Expressing feelings is generally frowned upon by most males. At a young age, young men receive the cultural message that they are to be strong and stoic and to shun emotions. Such an aversion makes deep relationships difficult, thus men find it difficult to make and keep friendship.
2. Males resist traditional fellowship opportunities or to be a part of any-thing other that athletics. Men find it hard to accept the fact that they need fellowship. Men may get together for business, sports, or recreation

(hunting and fishing), but they rarely do so just to enjoy each other's company. Centering a meeting on an activity is not bad; it is just that the conversation often never moves beyond work or sports to deeper levels.

3. Males have a greatly reduced number of positive role models to select from. The male macho image prevents strong friendships. The males' perceived aggressiveness and strength keeps men from knowing themselves and others.

4. Male competition occurs because men immensely enjoy it and see it as being a natural way of doing business. Men feel they must excel in whatever they do. This competitive spirit often develops a barrier to creating friendships.

5. Males don't like to ask for help because they perceive it as a sign of weakness. Others simply don't want to burden their family or colleagues with their problems. In the end, male attempts at self sufficiency rob them of fulfilling relationships.

6. Males have unrealistic priorities that often elevate the importance of physical things at the expense of creating meaningful relationships. Success and status is determined by material wealth rather than by the number of close friends.

Young men often limit their friendships and thus narrowly define their own identity. The more a man builds his identity around a small portion of his life such as vocation, family, or career, the more vulnerable he is to threats against his identity. This leaves these males more susceptible to experience a personal crisis all alone. A male who has limited sources of identity is considered by experts in a much more fragile stage of life. Males need to broaden their basis for self identity. They need to see themselves in several roles rather than just as an athlete, just as a scholar, just as a teacher, just as a salesman, just as a husband, or just as a male.

Far too many adults have failed to interpret the extent of the psychological depths that young men have sunk to over the past two decades. It is as though most people seem to neither understand nor care about their plight. Tupac Shakur summed it up nicely when he penned the poem "Sometimes I Cry." This poem talked about the pain and degradation experienced by today's young men who often find life too difficult to carry on. This generation of young men has no one to care or to confide in because adults seem far too busy to acknowledge their suffering. Young men are indeed crying inside and yet secretly hoping for some personal validation from the world.

More and more American parents and students desire smaller class sizes and more intimate school settings. We have come to realize that big is not always better. Large schools may be good for reaching economy of scale and generating successful sports teams but, not for nourishing the individual human soul. Why is it that boys choose to isolate themselves as opposed to being a part of the whole school community? A bigger issue to examine is what can be done to bring them out of this self imposed malaise?

CROWDED LONELINESS

Loneliness is not just a problem of a few eccentric individuals. Loneliness is endemic to our modern, urban society. In rural communities, although the farm houses are far apart, communities are thought to be very cohesive and strong. People are physically very close to each other in our urban and suburban communities today but, emotionally very distant from each other. Close proximity does not translate into close community.

The term crowded loneliness has generated much research and discussion over the past fifty years. Its prominence is attributed to the breakdown of natural community network groups such as relatives, PTA, civic clubs, church, neighborhood and other community minded groups. Americans are known for creating casual relationships with a number of people. Twenty percent of our country moves from one dwelling to another each year.

Research suggests that if people think they are moving, they won't put down roots. People don't see the importance of reaching out and connecting with other people. This results in crowded loneliness being a large part of more and more of America's citizens today. Generalizations abound about the patterns of people who are lonely living in population centers:

1. The displacement of people who move repeatedly? It is estimated that the average American move about 14–18 times in his lifetime. This average is much lower in many of our industrial nation counterparts.
2. The displacement that occurs when communities undergo upheaval. The accelerated population growth during the baby boom years along with urban renewal and flight to the suburbs has been disruptive to previously stable communities. America's recession has greatly reduced the building boom we experienced over the past fifty years which has limited these large movements of people.
3. There is the displacement from housing changes within communities. The proliferation of multiple-dwelling units in urban areas crowd people together who frequently live side by side in anonymity. The suburban sprawl lends itself to anonymity.
4. The inflexibility of work schedules that increases isolation. The continuous operation of factories and offices dominate an area's economy

which leads to neighbors remaining strangers. New technology allowing people the work from home reduces human interaction.

5. The reduction of the nuclear family. The tremendous growth and acceptance of divorce as a new norm. The steady rise in the number of broken families and the dramatic increase of the older population living apart from the younger heightens social isolation. All of these notions have led to a decrease in relationships contributing to this growing crisis in loneliness.

These various characteristics of loneliness paint a daunting picture. Establishing healthy relationships will become more and more important as we move further into the 21st century.

Why do people choose to isolate themselves? Researchers note that one in four American have nobody with whom to discuss personal issues? Modern society has made it far too convenient for males to isolate themselves and to only be approached through casual networks such as emails, instant messaging, and social networking web-sites. We must promote the basic need for developing close friendships and the value of interacting with people from different generations.

DO ADULTS REALLY UNDERSTAND?

Adults must take the time to attempt to understand teenage language so they can understand what is going on in their lives. This is a huge problem in our public schools because not enough adults understand the language or true feelings of male students. We have interpreted their stoic appearance as one of not caring or indifference about what is going on in class. We must at least act like we understand when making the effort to bridge the huge communications divide. This tremendous gap we face today cannot be overcome without a dramatic shift in adult thinking. The following is a list of words that have little in common with the meanings that middle class teachers are accustomed to.

A few examples of the test of teenage slang: What do the following words mean to you?

- All Good Home Slice (good friend)
- Bank (money)
- Ink (tattoo)
- Bling (money, jewelry)
- Kick It (hanging out)
- Bomb (good looking)
- Not Even (you have no idea)

- Buggin (getting on nerves)
- On the Creep (fooling around)
- Cake (money)
- Otay (OK)
- Chill (relax)
- Off the Heezy (off the chart)
- Crib (home)
- Shady (underhanded)
- Dope (real cool)
- Sick (super cool)
- Down (alright)
- Snap (I get it)
- For Real (I agree with you)
- Stupid (out of touch)
- Spinners (cool rims on a car)

Language is born in relationships. Non verbal communications is also very important to males. The following are a few of the male non verbal cues.

- A half nod—bye
- Half smile—Hi
- Shake hands—good job
- Wink—good luck
- Nodding head up—hello
- Rolling eyes—annoyed or I can't believe that
- Staring at some one—they need to be quiet
- Shrugging shoulders—I don't know
- Nod—What's up?
- Pounding your fist—emotional expression
- Pounding someone else's fist—good job
- Moving open hand back and forth—Maybe
- Tapping of pen or pencil—anxious, lots of nervous energy
- Rising of eyebrows means the affirmative to Alaskan natives
- The OK physical gesture means something obscene in Europe
- Silence is a gesture of respect in Asia
- Direct eye contact is a sign of respect in the American culture
- Saying hello with a nod is not always rude

A second poem by Tupac Shakur titled "In the Depths of Solitude Dedicated 2 Me" highlighted the often confusing, uncomfortable corner that the American electronics industry, and the written press have painted young men into. The poem discusses that dilemma young men face in deciding what course of action to take in their hyper speed lifestyle each day. On the one hand they just want to be accepted but, on the other they want to be respected. These important decisions are unfortunately, made in isolation, without the benefit of wise, caring adults.

THE PRISON INDUSTRIAL COMPLEX

It now seems as though there is some conspiracy to rob many young men of any positive hope they have for their future. We must look objectively at the growing body of evidence that frames this mounting problem. This conversation often centers on things like the "Third Grade Failure Syndrome." Let me explain what has been happening in America over the past 50–60 years. The Prison Industrial Complex is a vast network of businesses that generates billions of dollars of profit at the expense of boys and young men who have not mastered America's educational system. These are the students who begin school with good intentions but, for a variety of reasons fail to pass the third grade reading portion of the CRCT (Criterion-Referenced Competency Tests).

The Prison Industrial Complex can use this data to project, with a great degree of accuracy, how many prisons and prison beds to build in preparation for this failing group. They project that these young men will be incarcerated by the time they are 14–18 years of age. This is essentially a self fulfilling prophecy. This is some of the most accurately disheartening forecasts that can be made about young people. Profiting on the backs of our failed public educational system seems like an unfortunate and misguided use of data, statistics, and resources.

Research shows that it now cost American taxpayers somewhere in the neighborhood of $50,000+ per year to house prisoners. It seems to this author that it would be a better investment for America to spend the $10–15,000 per year on the front end to provide a quality education for young people than to wait on the back end once students have failed. We must think about all the lost potential that is wasting away in jails and prison cells within our nation. The expertise of the Prison Industrial Complex can forecast the future of our boys with great accuracy. During the past two decades, roughly a thousand new prisons and jails have been built in the United States.

In spite of this increased building trend, America's prisons are more overcrowded now than when the building spree began. The inmate population continues to increase by 50,000 to 80,000 people per year. Statistics suggests that 70% of the prison inmates in the United States are illiterate. Prison construction in the United States has experienced unprecedented momentum over the past three decades. They are viewed as job creation centers. Since 1991, the rate of violence in the United States has fallen by about 20%, while the number of people in prison or jail has risen by 50%.

It has been said that a government's budget is not only a statement of priorities, but also a reflection of a society's values. It has been noted that the State of California's proposed budget reveals priorities that appear to be out of sync with the best interest of its citizens. California is spending almost an equal sum for prisons as it does for its public colleges and universities. It has been projected that over the next five years, the state's budget for locking up people will rise by 9% annually, compared with its spending on higher education, which will rise only by 5 percent. By the 2012–2013 fiscal years, $15.4 billion will be spent on incarcerating Californians, as compared with $15.3 billion spent on educating them.

There is much research about how the prison system continues to grow at the expense of funding K-12 education. Some experts insist that this has led to a predictable flow of school to prison pipeline with undetectable lines separating the educational and criminal justice systems. Police have become an increasing presence in public elementary, middle and high schools. Schools are forced to spend millions of dollars to hire their own police forces or contract with local authorities. Many kids typically pass through metal detectors before being allowed into the building, under surveillance by video cameras in hallways and subjected to random searches of their backpacks and lockers.

There is a new sense of intolerance with children. Officials no longer tolerate behavior that is considered outside the norm. Students in the past were able to cool off in the principal's office but now these same students can expect a trip to jail. Children not old enough to drive have been arrested for behavior ranging from throwing a temper tantrum to talking during school assemblies and violating the dress code. Zero tolerance has adversely impacted boys.

There is almost uniform agreement among experts that traditional public school education is strikingly deficient in addressing the sensitive needs of 21st century poor students. One must fully understand the student's environment before designing programs that promote reading, writing, and arithmetic. This suggests that we should somehow embrace the whole child concept as we progress further into the 21st century.

There are some who note that the high school experience marks the beginning of the "coming of age" period during which young people transition from adolescence to adulthood. This is the period when young people become more independent and competent learners. They establish good work habits and begin to think seriously about their future. The success of this transitional period will be instrumental in determining their success by the time they arrive at their mid-20s. There is a growing group of young people who learn a more discouraging set of lessons.

They come to see secondary school as irrelevant, available jobs as demeaning, and their prospects and choices as diminishing. These students drop out of school at alarming numbers and separate from school with little thought about the impact on the quality of life they can achieve. These groups of young people (15–20%) are considered unemployable.

The percentage is even greater in our largest urban centers where large high schools attended almost entirely by minority students are losing half or more of their students between ninth and twelfth grades. There has been a great deal more recent research regarding the burgeoning drop out problem. The Schott Foundation for Public Education Executive Summary 2008 provides some interesting dropout data about all fifty states.

Obtaining drop out statistics is often not a single and easily countable act. Systems often generate ambiguous and misleading data to discourage one from pursuing a true picture of this enormous problem. The dropout numbers point to an increasing alienation of children who are completely turned off about school.

One of the biggest challenges that many young men face today is what they should do after leaving school. It has been mentioned on numerous occasions that far too many young men do not believe that they will live beyond the age of 25 so they fail to adequately prepare for life. The following information is designed to offer some standard advice. It is not specific, but it does force individuals to develop a dialogue and make choices about what is important in their personal lives.

TRANSITIONING AFTER HIGH SCHOOL WHAT NEXT?

Habit 1: Be Proactive

Characteristics of a Proactive Person:

1. Respond according to your values.
2. Accept responsibility for your own behavior.
3. Refocus on your Circle of Influence.

Reactive Behavior: Reactive people allow outside influences (moods, feeling, or circumstances) to control their responses.

Proactive Behavior: Proactive people use the margin of freedom to make choices that best apply their values. Their freedom to choose extends as they wisely use the space between stimulus and response.

Example: Victor Frankl, a Jewish prisoner held in a concentration camp during World War II, discovered that the proactive choice of attitude is the last of the human freedoms.

"We who lived in concentration camps can remember the men who walked throughout the huts comforting others, giving away their last piece of bread. They may have been few in number, but they offer sufficient proof that everything can be taken away from a man but one thing: the last of the human freedoms–to choose one's attitude in any given set of circumstances, to choose one's own way."

—Victor Frankl

Accepting Responsibility

When we blame and accuse others, we are reactive. We focus on the weaknesses of other people and get so involved in their disturbing behaviors that we forfeit our power to think, feel, and act in our best interest. By exercising proactively, we don't let others' weaknesses drive our decisions. In spite of other peoples' actions and dispositions, we make choices according to our values, purposes, and vision.

The Four Human Endowments of Proactive People:

1. Self Awareness: Examining thoughts, moods, and behaviors.
2. Imagination: Visualizing beyond experience and present reality.
3. Conscience: Understanding right and wrong, and following personal integrity.
4. Independent Will: Acting independent of external influence.

   Circle of Influence: A person's circle of influence includes those things he or she can affect directly.
   Circle of Concern: A person's circle of concern comprises all matters about which he or she cares.

Expanding Your Circle of Influence

The circle of influence is like a muscle that enlarges and gains elasticity with exercise, but wastes away with lack of use. When people focus on things they can influence (their emotional bank account with others) they expand their knowledge and experience, and they build trustworthiness. As a result, their circle of influence grows. However, when people focus on things they cannot control, they have less time and energy to spend on things they can influence. Consequently, their circle of influence shrinks.

Proactive Language vs. Reactive Language

"I choose to go."	"I have to go."
"I control my own feeling."	"He makes me so mad."
"Let's explore alternatives."	"There's nothing I can do."
"I can . . ."	"If only . . ."

OUR VISION SHAPES OUR FUTURE

Many people gain a sense of who they are from the opinions, perceptions, and paradigms of the people around them. They allow circumstance, conditioning, and the social mirror to mold and form who they are and what they achieve. The most effective people, however, shape their own future. Instead of letting other people or circumstance determine their destiny, they mentally plan and then physically create their own results. What they have in their mind shapes their future.

Some international scholars note that the rest of the world is counting on America for leadership in resolving the issue of working effectively with young men. Unfortunately, other countries including England, Canada, Jamaica, Brazil, and South Africa are adopting 20th century American social policies that encourage the incarceration and destruction of young men. This is leading to a world-wide catastrophe. The general community has chosen to remain on the sideline as this issue remains largely unaddressed. Little is being accomplished while the future lives of boys are being destroyed in record numbers. Many of the schools that young men attend prepare them with skills that will make them obsolete before, and if, they graduate.

The following recommendations were strongly suggested as solutions to these challenges of boys:

Short Term:

1. Teach all boys to read at grade level by the third grade and to embrace education.
2. Provide a variety of positive role models for boys.
3. Create a stable home environment for boys that include contact with their fathers.
4. Ensure that boys have a strong spiritual base.
5. Control the negative media influences of boys.
6. Teach boys to respect all girls and women.

Long Term:
1. Invest much more money in educating boys as we do in locking up young men.
2. Help connect boys to a positive vision of themselves in the future.
3. Create high expectations and help boys live into those high expectations.
4. Build a positive peer culture for boys.
5. Teach boys self-discipline, culture and history.
6. Teach boys and the communities in which they live to embrace education and life-long learning.

Recent research has noted that when boys enter first grade they express positive feelings about themselves and their schooling, but by the second grade students' stories express negative concepts about the teacher and the school environment. There is widespread cynicism by the time boys become fifth grade students. It is generally thought that upon entering school in primary grades, boys possess an abundance of enthusiasm and are eager to learn. That intellectual interest is replaced by apathy by the fifth grade. The primary grades have traditionally been viewed as a more nurturing environment than the upper grades.

In early childhood education much of the activity is child-teacher centered. It is much more interactive in scope. In primary grades, boys progress and thrive at the same rate as their counterparts until the third grade failure syndrome. Many of America's boys never survive the effects of this experience. The achievement rate of many boys begins a downward spiral that extends until the end of that child's academic career.

Much discussion has been generated regarding peers and peer pressure. One researcher described how two students were tested utilizing two different models of friends' influence on the development of delinquency in disruptive young men. This research suggested that adolescent males are strongly influenced by their friends. The assumption was made that students who get involved with delinquent friends are more susceptible to becoming delinquent themselves.

Research was generated regarding whether or not friends actually played a causal role in the development of delinquency? This question remains largely unanswered. There are a number of different theoretical models proposed that account for a friends' apparent influence. One model, the Peer Influence model, views friends as causal, whereas a competing model, the Individual Characteristics Model, views friends as non relevant.

The Peer Influence model suggests that ineffective parenting leads to association with deviant friends which, in turn, leads to delinquency. A young man's association with deviant friends is seen as a necessary component linking ineffective parenting and later delinquency. This model rests upon evidence that most adolescents become involved with delinquent peers before they become delinquent themselves. Their involvement with deviant peers predicts the level of delinquency even after controlling for prior delinquency. For some youths even when delinquency preceded association with deviant friends amplified previous levels of delinquency.

Oppositional-aggressive hyperactivity occurs when disruptive children join together in cliques, their behaviors escalate and diversify. Proponents of this aspect of the Peer Influence argue that deviant friends reinforce and model antisocial attitudes and behaviors. This may be interpreted to mean that disruptive children co-influence each other toward delinquency. This perspective attributes a causal role to deviant friends, except that this role is mostly operative for disruptive boys.

Peer pressure is an important influence on a young person's attitude and behavior. Peer pressure influences a teens' wardrobe, their music, their leisure activities, and their choice of friends. Peers offer independence from the family, acceptance, a sense of personal worth, and support in times of confusion, models for appropriate conduct in a complex world, and social identity.

Many factors affect how peer influence feels and how the individual will respond to its force. The group enhances the adolescent's sense of self-esteem. At one time or another, many adolescents choose to go along with group expectations in exchange for having their need for association met. Peer groups hold a very influential place in adolescent life because they give their members the qualities that young adults seek. Peer groups offer independence from parents, acceptance and approval from others, the feeling of confidence and worthiness, and they also offer social rules for interacting with other youth.

The peer groups hold out these gifts of enticement in exchange for conformity and compliance with group demands. Young people seek reassurance from going along with the crowd because they crave a sense of identity and a sense of personal worth. Young men should be cognizant of the people they hang out with. I am reminded of a poem that makes this all the more important.

It Is Better To Be Alone Than In The Wrong Company

It is better to be alone, than in the wrong company.
The quality of your life will improve by spending less time with people you now associate with.
When you accept mediocrity in others, it multiplies your own deficiencies.

Successful people are very intolerant of negative people.

Many of your friends will change as you grow and mature.

Some of these so called friends will not encourage you to go forward and prosper.

Some of these so called friends will only remain your friend if you hang back with them.

You must seek out friends that will help you reach your positive vision in life.

Remember that true friends increase the value not decrease the value in your life.

Never seek counsel from unproductive people who care nothing about your success.

These are the first people who will give you their own personal advice whether it makes sense or not.

You must be more selective about the people who help you make meaningful decisions in your life.

Resist exchanging ideas with people who are not going anywhere in life.

Wise men seek out like minded individuals who understand the value of true friendship.

You must associate with other Eagles who learn at an early age to soar to great heights in life.

Do not hang with wolves that only learn at an early age to run and howl.

A mirror is a reflection of a man's face but that reflection can provide a strong idea of what type of friends a man chooses.

We often become much like those we are closely associated with.

This poem summarizes a huge problem in American public schools today. We have failed to systematically address this festering problem of improving America's public schools and more specifically how to successfully address the gender problem. The United States began to see a pervasive pattern of intellectual decline of our young men about the time that our young women were beginning to make dramatic gains. This seemed to distract us enough that young men begin to drift academically and have been allowed to continue this self destructive pattern for most of their K-12 school years.

There exists a male crisis at every level of education. Young men continue to fall behind at ever alarming rates. We have the data but have failed to implement a systematic plan of action. Now is the time to revisit themes that prevent young men from academically excelling in America's public schools. The following are generalized observations about a boy's experiences while in school:

1. Boys are often treated like defective girls.
2. Boys are kinetic, maddening, and failing at school. Educators are just now attempting new ways to change the way they deliver instruction.
3. Boys love video games because when they lose, the defeat is in private.
4. Middle school boys typically use their brain less effectively than girls.
5. A boy without a father figure has to learn on his own a different type of relationship with his female teachers.
6. Boys need to be mentored by an older man to remind them that school is crucial to life.

Experts acknowledge that there are significant differences in the learning styles between genders. Since approximately 70–80% of all teachers are female, it is important for them to make the necessary teaching adjustments in public school classrooms if we are to properly address the boy crisis in America. The learning styles for boys are oftentimes very different from girls. We must stop the practice of labeling and treating boys as little more than defective girls. Today, far too many boys are experiencing mind numbing rejection and indifference from the very people who are being paid to nurture and develop them. Life in America is still very difficult for young men!

One of the more troubling pieces of information that has been generated in recent years is the quality of life and the life expectancy of young men. It is almost incomprehensible to find out that far too many young men do not believe that they will live past the age of 25. When putting that fact into perspective, it is no wonder that too many young men live for today and do not bother to invest in themselves and plan for their future. They rationalize that their environment and the negative things that go with it are inescapable. They believe that even public schools have abandoned them. It is hard growing up in their hardscrabble neighborhoods where life is often defined by who is the toughest or where only the physically strongest survive. Their neighborhoods and livelihood have little to do with intellectual curiosity and more to do with learning life survival skills.

Their neighborhoods require street smarts not book smarts. Their neighborhoods require little room for emotions and certainly not the compassion that until recently was found in our schools. It is little wonder that young men are not doing well academically. America must do a better job of teaching them the new game called 21st century School. We must teach them the value of acquiring the intellectual capital that will be necessary for them to be relevant participants in this global society! We cannot passively allow our boys to stop dreaming about their vision for their future! The consequences for our nation are much too dire!

A QUALITY EDUCATION SECURES A NATION'S FUTURE

Over the years much research has been generated about the significance of education and its impact on a nation's future. Experts have theorized a number of ways to evaluate and determine a nation's wealth over the past 500 years. The following are criteria used over the last few centuries to determine the strength of a nation:

1. During the 15th and 16th century it was the country with the most gold
2. During the 17th and 19th century it was the country with the most colonies
3. During the 20th century it was the country with the greatest industrial production
4. During the 21st century it was the country with the best schools.

There is little question that our world has changed over the past fifty years and that we all operate in a vastly different environment from the one of our parents and grandparents. The following educational ideas need to be brought up to 21st century standards:

1. Educator's work must be different and far more expansive
2. Educational tools must be different
3. Educational lines of communication must be different
4. Educational information must be different
5. Educational leadership must be different
6. Educational teaching must be different
7. Learning must be different in that it begins at earlier ages (2–5)
8. Images of children must be different, without built in biases with lower expectations.

There is a strong correlation between the quality of education and the personal achievement an individual attains. The world is continuously comparing nations and the educational achievement levels of those countries. The following are a few generalizations about the quality of schools in many industrialized countries:

1. The United States have high income jobs but low achieving schools.
2. Germany and Japan have high income jobs and high achieving schools.
3. China, India, South Korea have low income jobs but high achieving schools.
4. The developing countries in South America. Asia and Africa have low income jobs and low achieving schools.

If the current trend of American public schools holds true it would send an ominous sign to our business community. This would lead to their continued investment of new jobs overseas because of what they perceive as America's failed public school system. More and more of our jobs will continue to be shipped off shore until we radically upgrade the quality of education that is produced in our public school system.

There are several questions that need to be raised by all parties interested in the well-being and the future of the United States of America. One of the major questions that must be raised is why young men continuously under-perform in public schools? The following observations about young males have been generated over the past 30–40 years after closely watching this sometimes overwhelming national challenge. They are as follows:

1. Many boys lack self discipline
2. Many boys lack a cohesive family structure
3. Many boys lack a positive father figures in the home
4. Many boys lack consistent basic resources
5. Many boys lack the opportunity of attending quality schools
6. Many boys lack a real commitment to improve school districts
7. Many boys lack trained teachers and administrators with vision.

These are by no means the only reasons but, should begin an honest and open dialog to address and offer far reaching solutions regarding the state of young men in America's public schools.

Chapter 2

Rebranding the 21st Century Male

James Brown's popular 1969, hit "I Don't Want Nobody To Give Me Nothing, Open Up The Door and I'll Get It Myself" sums up the attitude that needs to once again be revisited by many 21st century males. Do not look for outside help before first helping yourself. Young men need to take advantage of the many opportunities that are available to them after carefully examining the issues. Young men need to show a stronger resolve, determination and creativity before seeking help from elsewhere. It was not that long ago that this song was the mantra of many socially conscious males who grew up during the 50s, 60s, and 70s.

We routinely did not ask anyone to assist us! We were expected to develop our own vision and ultimately to determine our own destiny. Almost all of my friends had their own personal set of goals that they diligently pursued. We competed against each other but also generously shared tips for success. The "at large" community celebrated our modest accomplishments with a great sense of pride. There was an expectation of excellence for individuals growing up during this time period.

Change can either be frightening or exhilarating to most people. It can be helpful or harmful. One thing for certain is its inevitability! The breakneck speed at which our lives adjust to the many nuances of 21st century change will determine our level and quality of life as we move further into this millennium. This author is convinced that young people accept change much easier than more mature individuals. Their lives have been characterized as the 'Microwave Generation' or Generation Y. They are generally described by the following characteristics:

1. They are accustomed to things moving at a very rapid pace.
2. This is the MTV generation.

3. This is the interaction generation.
4. They don't really value the things that older Americans hold near and dear.
5. They are more self reliant.
6. They believe in multi tasking.
7. They are more entrepreneurial in nature.
8. They like bending and breaking traditional rules.
9. They enjoy working with other creative people.
10. They are accustomed to getting things done quickly.
11. They value balance between work and play in their lives.
12. They acquire information from things other than books.

The outlook of Generation Y individuals is so very much different from their 20th century parents and adults. We consistently complain at the lack of conformity in our children, our students and our neighbors. They are not "mini me's. We should not be disappointed when we do not see a familiar figure in the mirrors of life when we hold this Microwave Generation Y up for public scrutiny. They are experiencing the same generational growing pains that we went through during our developmental stages. We must offer more patience and try to understand where they are coming from and more importantly, where they want to go.

There are those who ask why there is now a sense of urgency? The future of our country is at stake! We must begin to resolve the growing issues surrounding the successful transition of young males into responsible young adult citizens. Our economy will only grow with a workforce that capitalizes on intellectual acumen by the majority of its citizenry. The 20th century industrial and textile based jobs have long since disappeared. They have been replaced by jobs that demand an increasing knowledge, familiarity, and comfort level with technology. Change is inevitable and yet we see many instances of people refusing to acknowledge new and better ways of doing business.

MODERN MALE MANIFESTO

It is the belief of many that America needs to develop a Modern Male Manifesto. A handbook designed for 21st century successful men. This would be a public declaration of principles, policies, positions, and intent. There was a much publicized push to better support women and girls during the 1960s and 1970s. There is now a need to mobilize comparable policies, spirit and resolve for the young men of our great nation. There is a genuinely urgent need to redefine the roles of the modern day 21st Century Males.

The purpose of this movement would be to develop a set of concepts that enable many more young men to gain successful entry into a happier, healthier, and more prosperous global society. America has far too long sat back and let the media and others define the role of boys with little input from stakeholders. We have unfortunately and unwisely assumed that these sometimes negative unwritten rules of male engagement were not shared, and internalized by all young men. We now see the damaging impact this aggressive and unsustainable Hollywood version of manhood has on our sons.

There needs to be a more serious attempt to create a document that will contain the ideas and solutions from the very young men who have chosen to withdraw from today's challenges. Their lack of success can be generally attributed to the fact that no one has ever bothered to explain how the "Game of Life " is really played. This Modern Male Manifesto should clarify the issues and offer advice for those young men who too often reside in a state of intellectual paralysis. This book will explain how young men should behave regarding this very complex, relevant and critical challenges. We can no longer tolerate the days of placing blame on others for not being fully informed. Too many young male lives have been negatively impacted because of their lack of connectivity. One can examine the litany of recent articles that point to "The Boy Crisis in America" to understand that a national endemic is sweeping across this nation.

ATTITUDINAL SURVEY

A comprehensive on line web based questionnaire is suggested for all students to complete in order to develop some base line data regarding the state of mind of today's male students (www.edtransform.com). It takes approximately 10–12 minutes to take this test and the results will prove very valuable in designing strategies that work best in classrooms. We all know the importance of attitudes and how they shape how we think and feel about life. A few of the following questions will be analyzed for better understanding:

1. What does it mean to believe in the American Dream?
2. Do you respect authority?
3. Who are your role models?
4. Do you understand how to get ahead in your current school?
5. Do you work better by yourself or in a small groups?
6. Are you a risk taker?
7. Are you able to maintain focus on your academics?
8. Are you aware of the public perception about your age group?

9. Are you afraid of academic failure?

10. Do you believe that you will live past the age of twenty-five?

We need to continuously survey, probe and interact with our boys to gain personal feedback and to understand how they see themselves in the world today. No one seems to ever value our young men's opinion. One of the more than 64 questions included in this survey refers to the so called "American Dream." Unfortunately, many young men not only, do not know what that concept means, but believe that their life is snowballing toward the "American Nightmare". We need to assist them in redefining who they are and who and what they are capable of becoming after reaching adulthood.

REBRANDING THE 21ST CENTURY MALE

The plight of the young American males has been discussed, dissected, and perused over the last 30–40 years with adults telling the story through their cultural lens. There has been an avalanche of negative reporting and stereotyping that has sprung up and become an important topic for Fortune 500 companies to grapple with. Our homes, schools, work place settings, health care industries, politics, entertainment industry, athletic fields and our justice system has been dramatically altered by America's perception of young American Males.

It is this author's belief that the balanced, accurate reporting of males has never been a high priority in America's public schools. There has been too much emphasis on selling sensational, negative stories that it begins to sound more and more like the norm. Young males must begin to tell their own story in their own words!

They must be responsible for determining their own destiny and not be defined by some faceless reporter in print or on television screens across our nation. We must have a serious dialogue about rebranding the young male that allows for every stakeholder's voice to be heard and taken seriously. We must first begin by engaging the true stakeholders. I am referring to the millions of young males who reside in the United States.

WHERE DO WE BEGIN?

Branding is not a new concept to the business world. How would such an enormous task like rebranding a whole segment of the American population take place? Could a business model be appropriate for such a sensitive human mission? This author looked at several models and was most impressed with the volume of information generated over the past twenty five years. Many business efforts adhered to several basic themes.

Rebranding is a term that is often used to re-invent a specific product. While it is commonly used, the preferred term to evolve your brand makes more sense because you have a brand (personal reputation) that is already active and used.

It takes time to change people's perception and shift their ideas about you. Many experts suggest that you must begin the task by gathering the following information:

1. Find out what is your current brand or reputation
2. What attributes of your current brand do you want to keep and emphasize?
3. What attributes do you need to de-emphasize or to decrease?
4. What are different approaches that show those attributes increasing?
5. Which attributes will you start decreasing now? How will they be tracked?

The "Coke-A-Cola" name has an estimated brand equity value of over $70 billion, making it recognizable worldwide. The company basically sells sugar and water in a can. The greatest brand in the world is YOU! It has a much higher brand value than Coke. One must protect, nurture, and cultivate this reputation at all cost. We must brand ourselves before others do it for us. We must avoid at all cost allowing others to brand us. Individuals should have control in determining their reputation, the perceptions of others, their image, the intangibles, and ideas that other people have about them. The following is a helpful list of points to consider when engaged in creating a personal brand:

1. What's unique about you and how do you differentiate yourself from others?
2. One must position yourself clearly in the minds of others
3. One must be very deliberate about what you want others to think about you. Focus your message and your mission
4. One should be the picture of reliability and always project credibility
5. One must strive to develop brand loyalty
5. One must make emotional connections with your perceived customers

Many experts agree on three areas you need to focus on before attempting to develop a "Brand You" strategy.

Developing your brand: Rebranding yourself with new graphics and up to date information about boys will only get you so far. The American public is looking for a fresh approach. They want to know what has changed. We need to determine what new values and other attributes we want to highlight about boys. What do they love? What do they hate? What are they great at doing? What are they most proud of? What do they want to be? What is important and valuable to them? What do they want to be known for? These are basic fundamental questions, and yet, sometimes these are the most difficult to answer.

You cannot present the same old product dressed up in a newly designed communications package. This new product will serve as the basis for everything that connects people to your brand, both logically and emotionally. The new brand should resonate with the soul. Your image is important but an image is just a reflection on your brand and your core values. The idea of rebranding yourself goes far beyond promotion and marketing yourself to others. Experts agree that authenticity, consistency, and clarity are three pillars of a good brand.

Modern boys must look deep within oneself during this process and work hard to redefine who they are and what they stand for if this rebranding message will begin to resonate. It will be clear to others precisely because it is clear to you. A clear message is one that people can trust. Personal brands evolve overtime somewhat, but they remain essentially consistent at the core.

Packaging your brand: Businesses spend huge sums of money on the packaging of their goods and services! It is understood that people judge products (and people) based in part on appearance. First impressions are sometimes lasting impressions. A package for a physical product has to attract, inform, and persuade the customer to buy. The new package must be much more than an outer cover. The following list is used to help shape one's personal brand:

a. Your name
b. Your title
c. Your address
d. Your personal style
e. Your speaking style

Communicating your brand: Rebranding should always clarify and refine your position. The goal of rebranding should be to make it easier for customers and prospects to understand your value to them. Standing on the merits of your great work alone is not enough. People must know about you and your great work. They have got to meet you, see you. If you want people to talk about the wonderful things you do, then you must give them the opportunity to experience you first hand. This means attending meetings to network and getting involved in external organizations in your field. Some of the best contacts may come from unexpected places, but you will never know unless you get out there and interact with others.

Personal branding is extremely important in this world today! The market place is crowded and the labor market is competitive on a global scale. We must rise above the rhetoric and develop a clear idea about what we want to see in our 21st century young men. What makes you different? What do you have to offer that is totally different from your competition? One must dig deep inside yourself to determine your value. One must create opportunities to tell your story to the world once your message is crafted with precision.

The following information is designed as a business model but is modified as a starting point for discussion in rebranding the young American male.

Perspectives on Corporate Rebranding: Steps to Successful Corporate Branding

1. Establish and involve your key stakeholders both external and internal. Who knows more about young males than other young males and those who closely interact with them? These are the stakeholders. This is a common sense approach but many forget these simple and easily accessible sources of valuable information for the rebranding strategy.
2. Use external help to support change and to monitor and evaluate progress. Advance the corporate vision for what America wants to see in its young men. The corporate rebranding strategy is a productive method for advancing the corporate vision throughout the company. It allows the management to involve, educate and align everyone around the corporate objectives, values and future pathway.
3. Communication must be continuous, consistent and sustained through the use of new technology. Modern technology should play a large part of a successful boys rebranding strategy. Technology helps to gain effectiveness and improve the competitive edge of the new message. A well-designed and fully updated technological message is a must in today's working environment. This technological message has become increasingly virtual with employees working from home, from other locations and traveling across the globe.
4. Empower young males to become brand ambassadors. This ensures a broader commitment to change. The most important asset in a corporation is its people. They do interact every day with colleagues, customers, suppliers, competitors and industry experts to name a few. They interact with a number of people who may be disconnected to the corporations

through family members, friends, former colleagues and many others. These individuals can serve as the corporation's most important brand ambassadors as the word of mouth can be extremely valuable and have great impact on the overall image of the corporate rebranding process. Nike is a brand which is known for their efforts in educating and empowering everyone employed by the company to be strong brand ambassadors.

5. The communications plan must be designed to meet the needs of the different target audiences. One must create the right delivery system. The new and improved boys corporate brand is the face of the strategy and basically promises what all stakeholders should expect from the corporation. The delivery of the right products and services should be carefully evaluated on performance before any corporation starts a corporate rebranding project.

6. Focus communication by making your message concise and easy to understand. Bring the corporate rebrand to life through a range of well-planned, well-executed marketing activities, and make sure the overall messages are consistent, clear and relevant to the target audiences. Do not try to communicate every single point from the corporate rebranding strategy. Developing a selective approach will make much more impact using the same resources.

7. Monitor and evaluate the new message about boys at many different stages. Measure the rebranding performance and compare it to past results. Does it resonate with targeted markets? Rebranding should be accountable similar to corporate branding.

8. Adjust relentlessly and be ready to raise your own bar all the times. The landscape is changing every day in every industry. The boys rebranding efforts needs to evaluate and possibly adjust the corporate rebranding strategy on a regular basis. The rebrand should stay current, relevant, distinct and consistent throughout time. This ensures balance of the message. The basic parts of the corporate rebranding strategy like vision, identity, personality and values are not to be changed often as they are the basic components.

There are a variety of ways to interpret these themes depending upon your current stage of life. Wise leaders must decide to involve young male stakeholders who are considered leaders in their respective schools and communities. We should avoid the illusion of only soliciting the input of the so called good student. We need to actively pursue the voice of those young men who are potential dropouts as well as those individuals who have experienced modest success in the systems designed to help them. Young people rarely bite their tongue! They believe in telling the truth and are especially eager to tackle these complex but, exhilarating challenges.

The 2008 election of President Barack Obama provided stark evidence that this younger generation was now ready to assume an elevated status and become much more responsible for determining their own future. The actions of this generation proved that they wished to become equal partners in putting this country back on a sound, viable track. An overarching goal was to connect and build coalitions with like minded individuals regardless of age, color, or economic status. They provided strong evidence that they have the ingenuity and individual discipline to draft a comprehensive plan to rebrand the young American male.

It has been suggested that the organizational rebranding model has already been developed by President, Barack Obama. He empowered millions of individuals to develop personalized plans on their own to get a common message across to the masses. His philosophy resisted the notion that there was only one way of getting the job done. It was the sheer determination and ingenuity of a diverse group of millions of Americans to fulfill the destiny of rebranding 21st century America.

They believed that much could be accomplished by tapping into the creativity of a cross section of people rather than relying only on the traditional powers and institutions. It worked! Their main objective was not to sell the product but to generate a fascination with the brand. It was successful in getting the customer to identify with the world of the brand, creating brand awareness and providing it with a deep emotional bond.

America has been in the business of branding lifestyles for the past 50 years that have provided deep identities for many to assume. These forms of branding have at times influenced the core of our very being. They displace traditional ethnic and cultural traits and overwhelm the voluntary aspects of identities we choose for ourselves. We may choose to be an athlete for example, but we are branded as a Nike athlete by the Nike swooshes. We have experienced this over and over again and the media is excellent at reinforcing their interpretation of our new collective identity.

Recent research suggest that lifestyles are branded and brands stand in for lifestyles which take the place of character of the kind that once was the marker of identity. Every brand has a demographic market that it tries to attract. Our belongings and property often decides our position in modern society. The things we have, the places we shop or the types of lifestyles we live help to determine our brand. The following are examples of national brands that are easily identifiable:

Home Depot
Coca Cola
Urban Outfitters,
Gap

Banana Republic
Old Spice
Nike
Ann Taylor Fashions
Bed Bath and Beyond
AARP (American Association of Retired Persons)
Dell
College Athletic Team Logos
Baby Boomers
YUPPIES

Modern branding is so much more than an effective market transaction. Emotional branding defines a transaction as a one-night stand. It is never going to be as satisfying or rewarding as falling in love. A transaction makes the cash register ring once. A relationship makes it ring again and again. Selling takes on a new dimension when you put it in the context of a relationship. Emotional marketing also sometimes called emotional branding. It offers a glance at what some experts call social theory.

This concept distinguishes the old industrial economy from the new global economy. The old industrial economy is factory based and capabilities driven. It is production focused on manufacturing actual products. The new global economy is consumer based and consumer focused. It is more concerned with creating brands not manufacturing products.

Crisis in Masculinity

Much research has been generated in recent years that denote a crisis in masculinity. There are more recent attempts to dissect the modern 21st century male. We now know that they have very different attitudes and beliefs and that many of these beliefs are self destructive and anti establishment. There appears to be a growing generational communications gap because these new beliefs emanate from non traditional sources.

The modern day media has brainwashed young men into believing that being a man is determined by physical characteristics. Things like strong, independent, intimidating, athletic, and tough are terms often used to determine a man's veracity. Hollywood has done an exceptional job of misguiding a generation of young men who have allowed these executives to determine whether or not they are of "acceptable stock." Young boys start out early in life by avoiding at all cost the nicknames of wimp, wuss, fag, sissy, bookworm, or teacher's pet. All of these connotations conjure up negative perceptions that are to be avoided at all cost by boys.

Many of today's young men idolize athletes, actors, and entertainers such as rap stars, Rambo, Rocky and other violent action stars. The media construction of masculinity is built around ultimate and complete domination of one's opponent. Professional sports play a significantly important part in the lives of young men today. Today's media offers males very limited roles that are often built around violent and selfish attitudes including traits harmful to women. While femininity continues to be a topic widely discussed in America, the study of male masculinity needs to be moved to the head of the line in terms of thoroughly venting what the realistic meaning should be as we head further into the 21st century.

The definition of men is typically defined by modern media by such behaviors as competition, repression of fear and emotions, along with physical and emotional strengths. This is why many males consider the term cold blooded as an admirable trait. Many boys of color and those of lower socio economic status tend to encounter fewer alternatives for defining their masculinity than white boys or boys from higher socio economic backgrounds. This limited range of definitions available for masculinity encourages boys to define themselves in opposition to others, either as non-female, non-homosexual, or anti-authority. Many adolescent boys generally see female behavior as non acceptable.

The impact of this new belief system is that many boys have very few acceptable models of positive male adulthood. This results in many boys limiting their emotional connections because they interpret it as being unsafe or at the very least a threat to their masculinity. The overriding question of rebranding the young male is daunting at best. The debate over whether or not something must be done is very clear. The real question remains whether or not America has the will power and commitment to take the necessary steps to realize sustainable positive changes in our boys. We must seriously examine the change process regarding boys and how it may undermine our national security if not successfully implemented.

Individuality

By Charles Michael Choice
Be secure in who you are!
There can only be one you!

Those things that make you unique cannot be duplicated!
How you react to all you see, feel, touch,
and smell, represent your fingerprint in this life!

Your existence is purposeful, each and every second!
The Lord above decided to put you here and

that is why you must learn to appreciate
experiences that are good!

Have a short memory of those negative events that occur!
Rest assured there are more positives
than negatives in this world.
Live to the fullest, enjoy it all!

Our time here on earth is short,
he'll decide when your work's done!
Appreciate every step we take
until we walk no more!

EXAMINING THE CHANGE PROCESS

A sacred cow was once described as a plodding, bovine mammal of numerous stomachs and dubious intelligence regarded in some environments as holy in origin and therefore immune from ordinary treatment. The thoughtful book "Sacred Cows Make the Best Burgers: Developing Change-Ready People and Organizations" provided relevant analogies of how the business community is oftentimes guilty of reducing corporate profits. Some companies overly depend on old obsolete ways of conducting business that makes little sense in the 21st century. Ideas that a few years ago made millions were now seen as ancient and out of touch in today's modern world.

When 21st century adults hang on to the sacred cows of today it reduces one's abilities to think creatively. When we consistently fail to embrace innovation it ends up costing us large amounts of money and time. Sacred Cows are in our homes, business, churches, government centers, and especially in people's minds. These Sacred Cows are sometimes obvious but, at times can be difficult to detect like the background wall behind a Vincent Van Gogh painting. Many people and organizations are reluctant to abandon these once successful ideas and beliefs because these are the things that made them prosperous during the 20th century. We must systematically question our blind loyalty to the past.

The following are a list of current sacred cows that are undergoing revision or have been abandoned during the last twenty five years.

1. Job security with one company for life
2. Technology is a fad that will eventually go away
3. Forty hour work weeks with vacation time off for every employee.
4. Remain independent at all costs.
5. Top down management with little input from workers

6. Short term solutions are better for a company's future
7. Big government is there to make our life better
8. There is typically one correct way to accomplish most task

Sacred cows were highly prized in stable environments. The 21st century will continue to be ambiguous with large degrees of uncertainty at best. Change occurs daily in the lives of successful businesses. We must continuously prepare for global competition where there is a strong urge to just survive at the expense of everyone else. One has to continuously deal with more demanding and sophisticated international customers, more stringent governmental regulations, and new technological breakthroughs that seem to be introduced by the hour.

Many businesses are attempting to reinvent themselves while worldwide economic conditions remain in a state of flux. They have restructured and downsized as much as possible. Their own survival depends on how they assess the myriad of intriguing ideas that have bombarded them in recent years with the goal of creating a new corporate vision. There are consultants out there who will try to convince you that their equipment, their brand of products, or their corporate training will resolve your current dilemma.

The problem is much more than just selecting a plan! The key to success will be how an effective plan can be implemented. Years ago companies could possibly wait out these storms of change. This is no longer an option! Today's challenges require courageous leaders who relish being risk takers. These are the types of leaders who understand that you make significant progress by investing in your people if your goal remains to achieve sustainable change.

Throwing money at the problem is not the answer! Adults must understand the urgency to reexamine and shift long held ideology and beliefs, sacred cows, into new and bold ways of addressing old problems. Leaders understand the significance of developing strong relationships with their people. This basic concept will go a long way in determining what companies succeed during the 21st century and which ones go out of business.

There are several fundamental skills that determine the overall success of change. There are some 21st century skill sets that individuals should possess in order to accomplish their personal and organizational goals. They are as follows:

Seven Traits of Change Readiness

1. *Passion:* A powerful emotion about a person, place or thing. Passion is the individual's level of intensity and determination.
2. *Resourcefulness:* People who are effective at utilizing whatever resources are available to develop plans and contingencies. They see more than one

way to achieve a goal and they're able to look in less obvious areas to find help. They have a real talent for creating new ways to solve old problems.

3. *Optimism:* People who have the ability to see the positive side of anything.

4. *Adventurousness:* People who are willing to seek out new or emerging ways of getting the job done. The inclination to take risks and the desire to pursue the unknown, to walk the path less taken. Adventurous people love a challenge. They tend to be restless and shun the comfort zone. They are easily bored by routine work.

5. *Adaptability:* People who have the capability to change according to the new circumstances. Adaptability includes flexibility and resilience. Flexibility involves ease of shifting expectations. If the situation changes their expectations shift right along with it. They adjust to the new circumstances with quickness and ease, so they rarely feel disappointed or let down.

6. *Confidence:* People who are free of doubt and have confidence in their innate abilities. A belief in your own ability to handle any situation that may come up.

7. *Tolerance for Ambiguity:* People who may not know all of the answers at this time but, are confident of obtaining them in the near term. No matter how carefully you plan it; there is always an element of indefiniteness or ambiguity where solutions do not appear until far into the process.

Change can be very difficult for some people to accept even when we know it is in their best long term interest. The world is rapidly changing and yet we continue to hold onto concepts that are dated and sorely out of touch. There are many theories about this notion and much research has been generated in recent years. We must all become better students and more comfortable with the change process if we expect to remain viable players in our local community and on the world stage. There are many who continue to resist change even when we know it is in our best interest. The following myths about change concepts are debunked by this author:

1. Crisis is a powerful catalyst for change: There is medical evidence that 90% of patients who have had coronary bypasses do not sustain change in the unhealthy lifestyle that deteriorates their severe heart diseases and greatly threaten their lives.

2. Change is motivated by fear: It is easy for people to go into denial of the bad things that might happen to them. Overeating and obesity are examples that fail to deter individuals from consuming far too many

calories. Compelling, positive visions of the future are a much stronger inspiration for change.

3. The facts will set us free: Our thinking is guided by narratives, not facts. When a fact doesn't fit our conceptual framework. The metaphors we use to make sense of the world are often rejected. Change is inspired by emotional appeals rather than factual statements.

4. Small, gradual changes are easier to make and sustain: Radical, sweeping changes are often easier because they quickly yield results and benefits.

5. We can't change because our brains become hard-wired early in life: Experts now believe that our brains have exceptional elasticity that continues learning complex new things throughout our lives, as long as we remain engaged and active.

Author and motivational speaker Zig Ziglar (Over the Top: Moving From Survival to Stability, From Stability to Success, From Success to Significant) has a wealth of inspirational quotes which accentuates the importance of change. They are as follows:

"When you change your world for the better, you have positioned yourself perfectly to change the world of those around you."

—Zig Ziglar

"If you don't like who you are and where you are, don't worry about it because you're not stuck either with who you are or where you are. You can grow. You can change. You can be more than you are."

—Zig Ziglar

"One definition of insanity is to believe that you can keep on doing what you've been doing and get different results."

—Zig Ziglar

"Far too many people have no idea of what they can do because all they have been told is what they can't do. They don't know what they want because they don't know what's available for them."

—Zig Ziglar

"Don't wait until you feel like taking a positive action. Take the action and then you will feel like doing it."

—Zig Ziglar

Young men must understand and recognize the importance of making adaptations that lead to successful change from a very early age. They must become so familiar and comfortable with life changes that it becomes second nature to them. They should begin to look to the future to help resolve many of their current problems.

Many noted researchers recommend that young men should limit their time with toxic people. They suggest that you separate yourself from the toxic people in your life and question if you really know who they are? They are people who are poisonous to your goals, health, and spirit. They are the people at your work, social events, and neighborhood who make you feel unsafe, uneasy, and/or insignificant. They are the people who bring you candy when you are on a diet or tell jokes at your expense.

They are the people who encourage you to involve yourself in inappropriate activities. Young men need to get rid of the toxic people in their life just as some people must rid themselves of toxic substances. They must rid ourselves of toxic people or at least limit their time with them as much as possible.

A young man can gain very little by associating with toxic people. These people want your time, money, ear, energy, and probably your self-respect. They want from you whatever they lack. They feel entitled to whatever they can steal. Some may be nice to you in many ways, but very toxic and disingenuous in other ways. We must be cognizant of what defines success. The ability to find motivation and continue to learn is an important characteristic of successful people.

If you are not adding to your knowledge, resources, health, spirit, and character, then these too will begin to diminish. If you are not moving forward, you are probably moving backwards. There are many who promote tough love advice for young men who are grappling with their personal journey of life. It is far too easy for young men to see enticing things on television or the internet screen and expect them to suddenly appear as their possessions with little effort expended. It doesn't work that way in real life. There is no progress without struggle! We must redefine the 21st century male's efforts that are needed to obtain anything of lasting value.

DELAYED GRATIFICATION

The definition of delayed gratification is the ability to wait for something that you really want and desire. Delaying gratification is a process of scheduling the pain and pleasure of life in such a way as to enhance the pleasure by meeting and experiencing the pain first and getting it over with. This has been the traditional 20th century creed to live by. This tool or process of scheduling has been discovered by many children quite early in life, sometimes as early as age five. For instance, occasionally a five year old when playing a game with a companion will suggest that the companion take first turn, so that the child might enjoy his or her turn later.

Anger is an example of an emotion bred into us by generations of evolution in order to survive. Balancing is the discipline that gives us flexibility. Extraordinary flexibility is required for successful living in all spheres of activity. We exhibit anger when someone attempts to encroach upon what we consider our territory. We fight back in order to prevent being taking advantage of or eliminated is a form of anger. Discipline means to instruct or educate, to inform the mind, to prepare by instruction in correct principles and habits; to advance and prepare by instruction.

> "Motivation is the spark that lights the fire of knowledge and fuels the engine of accomplishment. It maximizes and maintains momentum."
>
> —Zig Ziglar

One of the most important dimensions of improving the life of young males is to build up their self esteem. The following is a list of Commandments that young males are encouraged to live by:

1. Thou Shalt Not Hang With People Who Diminish You
2. Thou Shalt Always Seek Perspective Regarding Real Life
3. Thou Shalt Not Hang With People More Dysfunctional Than Yourself
4. Thou Shalt Maintain A Strong Body and Mind At All Times
5. Thou Shalt Be True To Your Feelings and No Permission is Required To Say No
6. Thou Shalt Never Give Less Than Your Best
7. Thou Shalt Not Be Preoccupied With What Others Think About You.
8. Thou Shalt Be Wherever Thou Art and Not What Others Think You Should Be
9. Thou Shalt Promote Thyself For the Rest of Your Days.
10. Thou Shalt Look like You Are About Something At All Times

My good friend, Mike Howard wrote "From Ordinary to Extraordinary: Success Begins Within." He believes that individuals should capitalize on OPK (other people's knowledge and OPE (other people's experience) and utilize OPN (other people's network). Mike uses the following word to generate some very stimulating conversation from his audiences. I am most impressed by Mike's questioning tactics on the following:

What does this word mean to you?
Opportunityisnowhere.

Upon first glance one would strongly suggest that it is a nonsensical group of letters. With further examination and input from others one could arrive at a variety of interpretations. There are basically two distinct ways to interpret this group of letters.

1. Opportunity is no where and
2. Opportunity is now here

I have worked with and observed Mike Howard when he delivers his highly motivating lectures and most young people overwhelmingly believe in the second interpretation. It is true that opportunities are now here if you indeed prepare yourself to take advantage of them. The best thing about living in the early part of the 21st century is that the opportunities will continue to multiply for those who begin to prepare themselves and anticipate the unexpected.

One must continuously examine the way we do things and make the necessary updates and adjustments. Today's 21st century workplace requires a new way of thinking! Embrace the changes or risk being swept under the rug! We are living in a time of great social and technological transformation. Clinging to outdated beliefs about work and life is a sure road to nowhere. The following is a comparison of new and old ways of thinking:

Old Belief # 1:   Change is to be avoided. Change is another word for loss.
New Belief: Change is exciting. Change is another word for opportunity.
Old Belief # 2:   Mistakes and failures are disasters
New Belief: Mistakes and failures are learning experiences.
Old Belief # 3:   What can you do for me?
New Belief: What can I do for myself?
Old Belief # 4:   Look for something or someone to blame when a problem occurs.
New Belief: Take responsibility for solving problems even those you don't create.
Old Belief #5:   Wait for "them" to tell me what to do.
New Belief: We know what needs to be done. Make decisions and take action based on the facts known at the present.
Old Belief # 6:   Identify with a job title.
New Belief: Identify with a team for which everyone works toward the same set of goals.
Old Belief #7:   It is not my job.

New Belief: I will pitch in where I can.
Old Belief #8:   Ask "Why?"
New Belief: Ask "Why Not?"
Old Belief #9:   Security comes from loyalty to your company.
New Belief: Security comes from having skills that are needed in the marketplace. Update your attitudes and skills as your employer's needs change.
Old Belief #10: There is no need to continue one's education after getting the job.
New Belief: Life involves continuous learning and retraining.
Old Belief #11: I am an employee. My current job is the only option and there are no choices.
New Belief: I am employable. My current job is my choice and is one of many options I have.
Old Belief #12: The company is responsible for its employee's future.
New Belief: I determine my own future.

These are painful lessons that millions of Americans are experiencing first hand as our economy continues to contract and countless businesses are downsizing at record rates. These are essential pieces of advice that should be embraced by young and old if they are to flourish in the 21st century.

THE CHEESE HAS MOVED!

A very simplistic but powerful book about the change process was written a decade ago. The book *Who Moved My Cheese* provided several common sense life impacting themes.

Characters: The characters in this fictional book were two mice called Sniff and Scurry and two little people named Hen and Haw.

The "Cheese" is what you want to have in your life such as a good job, a loving relationship, possessions good health and spiritual peace of mind.

The Maze is where you looked for that "Cheese." It was about personal satisfaction.

"Who Moved My Cheese" had several analogies that were extremely noteworthy that human beings could apply to their lives in the 21st century. Some of these desires are as follows:

1. Having cheese (meeting our desires) makes you happy.
2. The more important your cheese is to you the more you want to hold on to it.

3. If you do not change with the times, you can become extinct.
4. What would you do if you weren't afraid to pursue your dreams?
5. Monitor your dreams and beliefs often so you know when they are getting old.
6. Movement in a new direction helps you find current goals and desires.
7. When you move beyond your fear, you began to feel freer.
8. Imaging yourself enjoying new pleasures even before you find them.
9. The quicker you let go of old beliefs and desires, the sooner you find new ones.
10. It is safer to search in the maze of uncertainty than to remain in a hopeless situation.
11. Old beliefs do not automatically lead you to new pleasures in life.
12. When you see that you can find and routinely enjoy new pleasures, you readily change course.
13. Change happens because someone keeps moving the pleasures of life.
14. Anticipate change and be ready to take advantage of the pleasures of life.
15. Adapt to change quickly because the quicker you adjust the better off you will be.

This widely read book made the change process more pragmatic, relevant, and palatable for many people who would otherwise be set in their nonproductive ways. It is my belief that young males must redefine themselves without the interference and input of the media at large. It is important that young men do the work of self introspection and began to repackage themselves with reduced input from non stakeholders. I believe that one must consciously remove the Hollywood stereotypes that have far too long negatively characterized young 21st century males.

It is unacceptable that many of our young men have embraced and lived up to the questionable reputation that is prevalent on television, videos and in our daily newspapers. We must ensure that a systematic makeover of the current unproductive boys' model is radically changed into a new productive one with energy, vitality, relevance, consistency and morals. There are several successful business models available when one begins the difficult task that is the "Re Branding" process. We must generate a renewed resolve to assist and guide our young men into becoming contributing members of the United States and the world community.

Chapter 3

Mentoring and other Male Affiliations

I first heard the lyrics to "Lean On Me" by Bill Withers in 1972. It highlighted the importance of older, wiser men taking an interest and being responsible for mentoring, caring and nurturing the younger generation. This song recognized that young men were not yet strong enough to shoulder the enormous responsibilities of evolving into manhood without good guidance. The song suggested that one should not be so proud as to resist asking for help when it is critical to a person's success. We have not always fully embraced the true meaning of this song to provide counsel for any youngster who may need our help.

Young men need sound advice now, more than ever before. The old song "No Man Is An Island" is self explanatory. One cannot resolve these difficult 21st century challenges in isolation. The access to reasonable advice will prevent many young men from wondering aimlessly in their attempt to overcome significant life challenges on their own. Responsible adults can no longer afford to sit back and wait for things to improve. It is our obligation to help things get better! We have to engage young men and demonstrate to them the path to self determination.

Young men must develop more ownership for controlling and determining their own destiny! It is important that young men know that someone outside of their immediate household wants to invest in their future and to help them lead more productive lives. Building strong, effective, supportive communities is one of the big issues now facing America. Our nation has a rich history of valuing family involvement. We must come together with like minded individuals who share a vested interest in healthy, sustainable, community growth. A strong community benefits not only the individual but the greater society as well. People across all ages exhibit a sense of belonging which leads to a more productive life when we work toward this common goal.

It is important that young men be introduced to team sports, boy scouting, fine arts, technology and reading that is age level and interest level appropriate. The adolescent age is the time that boys begin to discover their innate talents, begin to cultivate their individual talents and collective interest. This is also the time they must begin to bond with other positive males outside their immediate household. It is the role of older men to encourage children to look toward the future and not be tied to outdated notions of the past.

There is a great poem that characterizes the role of the more seasoned citizen when setting the direction for younger males to follow. The Bridge Builder by Will Allen Dromgoole has many hidden messages. One of which is the notion that responsible adults must be generous with their time and should always be considerate of others. The older man in this poem crossed a steep river and immediately started building a bridge over it. He reasoned that other fellow travelers would have trouble crossing this same road in the future if he did not complete this task. The old man was confronted by a person who questioned him about building this particular bridge especially when he had already made it to the other side.

The old man replied that he was building it for others who would need to cross this same bridge in the future. His message was to do something beneficial for mankind with the time you have left on this earth and to leave a legacy that would benefit the youth. Civic minded men should internalize this poem and challenge others to think about the importance of becoming a mentor. They will not only enhance the lives of children but their own lives as well. We should all strive to better serve our communities and to leave a positive personal legacy. Creating positive footprints for others to follow should be an important goal for all of us.

LOOK TO AN INFLUENTIAL PERSON

We cannot expect America's young men to resolve the monumental challenges of growing up with little meaningful input from responsible adults. A young man's missteps in life can be much too severe and result in dire consequences to be left solely up to chance. It is the responsibility of each adult to do his part if we are to successfully address this generational issue. Our public schools can no longer shoulder the entire burden of raising and educating children all by themselves. Well intentioned citizens must step forward to develop real and lasting partnerships throughout this nation. The opportunity to get involved in the life of a young person does not cost a lot of money. It will however, require an investment of our time and wisdom if we are to adequately address these issues.

People influence others through their behavior, feelings, and lifestyles. There have been a number of people who served as sources of inspiration for many of us. The following exercise will help one discover the character traits you value most.

1. Who has served as a positive role model for me and has had a significant impact in my life? Why did that person have such a significant impact?
2. What qualities does this person possess that I would like to emulate?
3. What other qualities of character do I most admire in others?

It's important to determine if you are the right kind of person who can build a secure relationship with young people. You must be trustworthy and believable if you are to avoid destroying this relationship. Most people value a true friend that they can depend on to be consistent in their interactions. Everyone wants to have friends, but find them to be scarce when you intentionally look for them. When you go out in life to be a friend, you will be welcomed everywhere. You rarely completely change anyone. People will gravitate to you when you internally change yourself and become that special kind of person who automatically helps others.

Most young men want a friend who is friendly, dependable, and loyal, a friend who will stand by them in times of trouble. A fair-weather friend is someone who is always around when he needs you. A real friend is someone who is around when you need him and will never stand in your way except when you are falling. There is no greater compliment than when a young man proclaims that his real friends will always "have my back." This endearing term simple means that they have someone they can trust to support them with their life is need be

"Wise is the person who fortifies his life with the right friendships."

—Author Unknown

A hundred years from now it will not matter what your bank account was, the sort of house you lived in, or the kind of car you drove . . . But the world might be a better place because you were important in the life of a child

—Author Unknown

The significance of a caring mentor can not be underestimated. A mentor is someone who listens, someone who provides encouragement, and support along with positive reinforcement. A mentor is someone who nurtures and informally teaches. A mentor is someone who generates trust and a belief in his mentee.

—Author Unknown

Good mentors are needed by children of the rich and poor, minority and majority, one and two parent families.

—Author Unknown

Parents should always be thought of as a child's first mentor. Parents can either guide their children in the right direction with the goal of building self-esteem, or they can make life a far greater struggle for their offspring. All parents must realize that it is one of the most important jobs one will ever have. We must be outstanding mentors and role models to your children while they are young and continue this bond with them when they grow into adulthood. We must consistently "walk" the walk" as well as "talk the "talk."

A parent who demonstrates his love to his children will be able to hide many other deficiencies. Good schools and communities have always provided responsible teachers and coaches who have served as mentors to America's children. It is important that good mentors become a consistent presence in the lives of today's young people even as they transition into adult roles in life.

MENTORING PROGRAMS

There are many types of mentoring programs. Informal mentoring consists of the following components:

1. No time requirements
2. No regular contact between mentors and mentees
3. No assistance to the relationship by any organization or agency
4. No entrance criteria.

Evidence is not as consistent regarding this particular program because it often does not generate the commitment that children need from a responsible adult. If you say you are going to be there for a mentee (child assigned to the mentor) then you must be there. These young people have been disappointed far too often over their short lifetime. Please do not disappoint them again to avoid being thought of as just another adult who does not really care about their future.

Formal Mentoring is characterized by the following beliefs:

1. Long term, deliberate relationships
2. Third party (organization, schools, agency) leads the efforts
3. Minimum time requirements (1–3 hours per week)

4. Screening and matching of mentor and mentee process
5. Frequent and regular contacts between mentor and mentee
6. Support from organizations, schools, agency
7. Specific focus: social, career, employment, life, academic.

Experts suggest some type of mentoring program for the following reasons:

1. 21st Century students have fewer positive alternatives after school other than hanging out in unsupervised environments
2. 80% of students in the USA have working mothers.
3. 60–70% of boys and girls do not have active fathers in the home.

Mentoring skills that connect with young people:

1. Good communications skills
2. Being able to listen effectively
3. Responding in a way that a young person will listen
4. Being quiet while someone else is speaking does not constitute good listening.

Mentoring Skills work when the following occurs:

1. Try to understand someone
2. Learn something from someone
3. Help someone express his or her thoughts and feelings
4. Maintain eye contact
5. Reinforce students by nodding, paraphrasing and asking questions to clarify what has been said.

"A lot of people have gone further than they thought they could because someone else thought they could."

—Author Unknown

Developing Positive Self-Esteem

1. Children see themselves through the eyes of others. Boys are often told they are bad. If you see them as lovable and capable, it is a terrific first step.
2. Empathy: Find a common bond and empathize with how your mentee is feeling

3. No negativism: Praise your mentee. Give positive reinforcement. Try to find something they did well.
4. Opportunities and Options: Teach your mentee about the opportunities that are out there and about options that were available while growing up.

Rules for Boundary Setting

1. Set healthy limits on the amount of time you are willing to spend with your mentee and the level of your personal involvement.
2. Your role is not to rescue kids. You are there to be a role model and to help them develop skills for effective living.
3. Do not expect that your mentee will initially talk to you about personal problems. It is a successful relationship when it does occur.
4. Mentees often test the relationship. They may be unusually rude or irresponsible. The testing behavior may reflect the mentee's fear of abandonment by significant people.
5. Your mentee may be wondering when or if you will leave them.
6. Continuity of relationship is critical. Some mentees experience inordinate disruption in their lives and may move frequently from one location to the next.
7. When a mentee does something inappropriate, confront it directly but with sensitivity. Be honest and model an appropriate way to discuss this shortcoming.
8. Your mentee may dress, act, talk and look very different from you. Different does not mean better or worse. Making a value judgment based on outward appearance or different styles is a very relationship damaging thing a mentor can do.

Mentoring programs have evolved in our schools, workplace, churches, communities, and our prisons. We need to multiply this number so that each boy who seeks a connection with a more experienced adult should have one! Mentors are better able to understand what the pressures and challenges young people have to endure growing up in the 21st century. Mentors can now develop friends for life!

Public schools are in desperate need of responsible male adults because the students benefit as well as the adult who wishes to make a difference. The infrastructure is in place and it is a great opportunity for the business community to reconnect with public schools in America. The student-adult friendships that develop generally last a lifetime! The results are a win-win based on these general statistics:

1. 70% of students improved their overall academic grades
2. 70% of students showed higher levels of self-confidence, and self esteem
3. 60% of students had a better attitude about school.
4. 75% of students were better able to problem solve
5. 75% of students developed better oral communication skills with adults
6. 75% of students improved their in school attendance
7. 80% of students are able to make long term decisions about their future
8. 80% of students now believed they have a caring responsible adult to confide in.

"To the world, you may just be somebody. But to somebody, you may just be the world."

—Author Unknown

There are important keys to understanding and connecting with young males today. Steven Covey's book, "Seven Habits of Highly Effective People" highlighted the significance of creating lasting relationships between individuals. We must seek first to better understand these young men before we can expect to be heard and understood by them. Today's adults have little understanding of the multitude of hurdles young men have to go through in order to be valued and affirmed. Everyday life and circumstances have gotten so far out of sync in the lives of many young men that adults have to work hard just to conceptualize the challenges they face. A more comprehensive understanding must be in place before we will ever be able to assist boys through life's perilous journey.

"Kids don't care how much you know until they know how much you care."

—Author Unknown

One of the most important goals when working with young men is to encourage them to trust and believe in someone or something. The 21st century media has done a masterful job of destroying their sense of community. Adults must teach young men the value of networking. Some people are naturally good at networking and yet untold others need to work diligently to realize its importance. It is a slow process that takes time to develop but, it is essential that young men incorporate these habits into their daily routines. They are as follows:

1. Always seek quality relationships because a person who is willing to go the extra mile to help you is worth more than someone who consistently offers excuses.

2. You must be sincere and genuine and always approach people in good
   faith.
3. You must learn the value of staying in touch especially with the very
   busy schedules of the 21st century life. Learn to use the personal touch
   and not always rely on electronics.
4. Don't wait until you need some help before you begin to build your
   personal network. Stop pre-judging the long term value of the people
   we meet!
5. You must get out of your passive state and be proactive. Do not expect
   people to always come to you or to make the first move. It is not all about
   who you know! It is more about who knows you and more importantly,
   what they think about you.

There are millions of boys out there who have starkly similar needs.
One could easily become overwhelmed when you begin to consider
the enormity of the problem. How can we systematically address this
growing American dilemma? One suggestion is to bring focus groups
of young men together to generate solutions and to help them develop a
systematic network when addressing their own problems. This idea was
developed in January 2007, at Kennesaw State University, Kennesaw,
Georgia when the first of a series of 21st Century Male Leadership Conferences was developed.

The idea was to invite twenty-five individual Metro Atlanta high
schools to identify up to ten young men who have displayed leadership
potential in their building. We took those names and wrote a personal
invitation for them to come to the Kennesaw State University (Kennesaw,
GA) campus for a day of leadership development. The "Breakout Sessions" were conducted by male college students who were eager to share
their knowledge and background with slightly younger high school male
students. This was what could be called the trickledown effect. The male
oral traditions were now being passed down systematically from one generation to the next.

The initial conference brought together African American male high school
students and the exact same model was used to bring together Latino male
high school students. Female students from both high schools and middle
schools were later brought together with comparable results.

Each conference was attended by enthusiastic future leaders from a variety of schools who received the same information at the same time. A natural
bond began to develop between each of the K-12 students and their college
student presenters. A level of cooperation had already been established

between the adults and the college students. What better way to systematically develop a plan of action for a large group of potential leaders.

The conference vision was shared and the various high school leadership teams now had their marching orders and understood the value of a disciplined protocol when addressing the problems surrounding boys. The young men receive a great deal of positive attention from their school communities and gained a level of leadership training that had once been thought impossible to achieve in large numbers. This program model has now also been used to bring together upper elementary school student leaders with the same degree of success. One can gain additional information by going to Google and typing in Henry E. Holliday, Ph.D. You must scroll down to KSU leadership conference.

DEVELOPING MALE LEADERSHIP CONFERENCES

This is not a very complicated challenge. It does require someone with courage and vision that is very organized. The following steps are recommended:

1. Secure a safe and easily accessible venue (preferably on a college campus)
2. Develop a schedule for the day's events (2–4 hours and be specific)
3. Secure funding resources for the number of students who will be attending
4. Develop a series of regularly scheduled meetings for the conference leaders
5. Send out letters of invitation
6. Set up your breakfast and lunch menu and times (be precise)
7. Set up your security in detail (be specific)
8. Set up your transportation plan (car, bus, mass transit)
9. Select and train your student speakers for 'Break Out Sessions'
10. Secure tee shirts, wristbands, and certificates of participation from business partners
11. Set up and post the conference evaluation forms
12. Develop a list of post conference assignments (tasks) for students
13. Set up a post conference evaluation for school adult sponsors
14. Set up the date, time, and location for the next conference
15. Contact, set up and prepare to accommodate the press

The following forms and concepts have been successfully utilized for male and female conferences all across the United States:

Bagwell College of Education
Department of Educational Leadership

December 2006
Dear Parent/Guardian,

Congratulations, your son has been identified as a potential leader and selected to receive some very valuable leadership training on the campus of Kennesaw State University (KSU). We have all witnessed some of the alarming trends that have negatively impacted our young African American/ Latino male students. This is the first of many KSU Leadership Development Conferences where we bring young leaders from Metro Atlanta high schools together to collectively brainstorm issues and generate solutions for their respective schools and communities.

The January 30, 2007, seminar will be attended by African American/ Latino male leaders from 15–20 high schools in addition to many adult community and professional leaders who have a great interest and want to get involved. Your son/guardian is considered one of the leaders of his school and will gain additional knowledge and networking skills upon completion of this seminar. We are training your son to play a more prominent leadership role in his larger community. Our breakout sessions will be conducted by KSU African American/Latino male students who understand what is needed to be successful and has a better feel for what today's male high school students are going through. We have had unparalleled interest in this conference and hope that you agree that it is an important first step.

Kennesaw State University looks forward to hosting this exciting event and anticipates a new synergy that begins to systematically address the myriad of public school issues surrounding African American/Latino males who have been left to resolve their own challenges. Please feel free to contact my office if you should have additional questions.

Sincerely,
H. E. "Doc" Holliday, Ph.D. Assistant Professor, KSU
hhollidda@kennesaw.edu
678-797-2234 KSU
drheh@comcast.net
Google . . . Henry Earl Holliday

Roster of Participants

School ————————   Advisor ————————

Email Address ————————

School _____   Advisor _____

Email Address _____

	Name	School	Grade	Email Address
1.				
2.				
3.				
4.				
5.				
6.				
7.				
8.				
9.				
10.				
11.				
12.				
13.				
14.				
15.				
16.				
17.				
18.				
19.				
20.				
21.				
22.				
23.				
24.				
25.				

Kennesaw State University Contact Person

Name ————————   Major ————————

Email # ————————

Name ————————   Major ————————

Email # ————————

SURVEY
Leadership Development Conference

Instructions
Please complete all items in sections I, II and III of this survey. This survey was designed by Dr. J. Eric Tubbs (Kennesaw State University Associate Professor in the Department of Educational Leadership) to gather specific demographic data and to measure the participant's perception of the leadership conference. No signature is required as the respondent will not to be identified.

Section I: Demographics

1. School Level		2. Ethnicity		3. Gender	
Elementary	0	African American	0	Male	0
Middle	0	Caucasian	0	Female	0
High	0	Latino	0		
		Multiracial	0		
		Other	0		

4. Where you Live		5. Age		6. Grade Level	
Rural	0	12–14	0	6–7 8–9 10	0
City	0	15–16	0	11 12	0
Suburb	0	17–18	0		0
Other:	0	19–20	0		0

Section II: Personal Leadership Style
Based on your participation in this conference we would like to determine if the conference helped you become a better leader. In Section II below, there are 12 statements related to the leadership skills presented at the conference.

On a scale of 3, 2, or 1, with 3 being the highest, rank each statement listed below by circling the appropriate number.

After attending the conference I:

Can set personal goals	3	2	1
Can be honest with others	3	2	1
Can use information to solve problems	3	2	1
Can now delegate responsibilities	3	2	1
Can set priorities	3	2	1
Am sensitive to others	3	2	1
Can consider input from all groups	3	2	1
Can listen to others effectively	3	2	1
Can create an atmosphere of acceptance	3	2	1
Can consider alternatives before making decisions	3	2	1
Can accept mistakes	3	2	1
Can now be more tactful and flexible with others	3	2	1

Section III: Barriers to Learning

A.

B.

C.

D.

E.

As a student please list five things that gets in the way of learning:

Men of Distinction: Position Paper

Event Date: Tuesday January 30, 2007
Time: 9 am to 1 pm
Place: Kennesaw State University, Student Center Rooms C–E
Theme: "Leadership Development for African American/Latino Males"
Sponsors: KSU Office of Minority Student Retention, AAMI; KSU Distinguished Black Gentlemen/KSU Latino groups and others.
Purpose:

1. Train high school African American/Latino males to become more effective leaders in their schools and communities.
2. To teach more effective leadership skills to students
3. To teach networking ideas and how to cooperate with other regional schools
4. To train college and high school students how to develop coalitions to work toward common goals.
5. To give males a first hand exposure about the realizations and expectations of college life.
6. To teach high school males how to develop positive grass root organizations.
7. To develop a network of advisors with the intent to open lines of communication between schools and the larger community.
8. To develop a list of projects that can be replicated by other schools.
9. To share money making ideas that can be replicated
10. To develop an awareness of the electronic mentoring program (EMP).
11. To hear and meet many gifted and talented adult role models from the community at large
12. To develop an awareness of self-worth and self-respect
13. To expose students to their heritage, history, and culture
14. To develop public speaking skills.

Background Information:

There is no question that there is a large disconnect between the African American/Latino Males and the American Society. This is especially apparent in many public schools today. The problem has been allowed to grow exponentially. There are now a significantly reduced number of African American/Latino males graduating from high schools and enrolling in colleges across the United States. The Georgia Board of Regents recognized this fact and initiated the African American Male Initiative (AAMI) in 2005 with the goal of recruiting and attracting more capable males to college campuses. The KSU "Leadership Development Think Tank" is designed to do the following:

1. To bring in African American/Latino males from a number of Metro Atlanta high schools to train them on basic leadership qualities.
2. To allow male college students to host, interact, and train younger students.
3. To allow college, high school, and ultimately middle school students to interact with professional African American/Latino males to learn more about future careers.
4. To assist KSU in developing a Regional Center for the research of African American/Latino males

5. To develop a systematic method of identifying and training quality male mentors for the electronic mentoring program (EMP)
6. To provide a regional opportunity to connect the dots and bring together all of the various programs assisting African American/Latino males into one more effective clearinghouse where ideas and resources are pooled together toward a common solutions.
7. To develop an academic action plan for each high school.
8. To suggest a list of social action activities for each school to complete:

   a. Community or school service project (feed the hungry)
   b. School improvement academic project (tutorial project)
   c. School environment improvement project (international festival)
   d. School climate safety project
   e. Community school to work project
   f. Aids awareness project
   g. Drug and alcohol prevention project
   h. Self-esteem and role-play project

This Leadership Development Seminar will occur twice a year (during each semester) on the KSU campus. The African American/Latino male stud ents of KSU are committed to partnering with regional high school and middle schools to assist in making their schools more effective and relevant during the course of the year.

RSVP: Please select 6–10 young men from your school to attend this seminar. All participants must RSVP their name, school, grade, and email # by Dec. 4, 2006 so that programs can be printed and food ordered.

Program/Tuesday Jan. 30, 2007
Refreshments
Open Remarks
Purpose of Seminar
Guest Speaker
Break
Break out Sessions (led by college students)
Lunch (announcements) Survey Completed
Tour of Campus
Review of Day (led by high school students)
Advisor's Feedback (high school)
Photo Opportunities/Interviews/Dismissal

Contact Information:

Dr. H.E. Holliday, Professor Kennesaw State University, 678-797-2234 KSU hhollida@kennesaw.edu www.edtransform.com1621

WHAT REALLY MAKES A DIFFERENCE?

It is interesting how some people always manage to perform well while others don't ever seem to get ahead regardless of the many resources within their grasp. Why are some individuals, some schools, and some communities faring better than others? Several experts have written extensively about the differences between companies that go on to become exceptionally prosperous and those who do not. This author has taken a business analogy and applied it to American public schools and males in particular for a comparison. Good is really the enemy of great. This might be one reason why there is little evidence of greatness in American public education. Far too many of our schools eagerly settle for just being good and never extending themselves to strive for greatness!

We don't have an abundance of great schools because we have conditioned ourselves that it would require too much effort which means that we routinely settle for average schools. We don't have great government because we settle for good government. Few people attain great lives because it is just so easy to settle for a good life. The vast majority of companies never become great because the vast majority become satisfied with being ordinarily good. The quality of leadership within schools determines their success in attaining lofty goals. The skill set for good to great leaders in our schools is a person who has passion, a sense of personal humility and the will power to implement change for the better.

These individuals are thought to be scholarly consensus builders and not ego centric leaders. Good to great leaders understand the importance of setting a clear new inspiring vision. You must first get the right people on the bus in the right positions before your intended destination can be realized. The direction of the organization has a lot to do with its culture. All businesses have some form of discipline, but precious few have a culture of discipline. This is important because when you have disciplined people, it lessens the need for strict organizational hierarchy and reduces bureaucratic controls.

Technology has a more robust role in good to great schools and companies. Technology should never be viewed as the primary way of launching a transformation. It is a tool to assist in day to day work! Most effective good to great leaders possess a non negotiable belief that their efforts will ultimately be successful in the end. They know that that they must confront their most compelling challenges if they are ever to reach their true potential. They are relentless in their pursuit from good to great, even when success comes in small doses, until a major breakthrough takes place.

FIRST WHO . . THEN WHAT?

America has come to a point in its history when we cannot afford to wait on others to resolve its 'Boy Crisis'. There are so called experts who would have us study the problem until more data is available. There are others who pronounce that you're either on the bus or off the bus promoting change.

The executives who ignited the transformations from good to great did not first figure out where to drive the bus and then get people to take it there. They first got the right people on the bus (and the wrong people off the bus) and then figured out where to drive it. They believed that getting the right people on the bus in the right seats, and the wrong people off the bus that the organization would end up in a much improved place that offered better opportunities to achieve greatness.

There is no more poignant thought or piece of advice that can be shared with young men than the following poem "The Company You Keep." This poem discusses the importance of always being aware of whom you hang out with because it goes a long way in defining who you really are. You should never develop friendships with fools or selfish people because it is typically built on a tenuous set of foundations. One should always seek friends with good character and virtues because they will have a positive impact on your life.

Man has a tendency to become like those with whom you closely associate for the good and the bad. The less you associate with some people, the more your life will improve. Any time you tolerate mediocrity in others, it will increase your mediocrity. One consistently important attribute in successful people is their impatience with negative thinking and negative acting people.

Our friends will change as we grow older. Some longtime friends will not want you to progress and move on. They will want you to stay where they are. Friends that don't help you climb will want you to crawl. Your friends will help you realize your vision or choke your dreams. We must always be mindful that those that don't increase you will eventually decrease you. Do not seek counsel from unproductive people. Never discuss your problems with someone incapable of contributing to the solution. One must first examine their track record before believing anything they have to say.

Only allow proven friends the right to offer advice about the direction of your life. You are certain to get the worst of the bargain when you exchange ideas with the ineffective people. Do not follow anyone who's not going anywhere. Spending quality time with uplifting people is equivalent to making a substantial investment in your future. One must always be vigilant about where you stop to inquire for directions along the road of life.

Chapter 4

Families

Marvin Gaye's "Inner City Blues'" thought provoking lyrics written back in 1971 are still very much relevant today. It continues to sum up the state of mind of far too many young men in America. It depicted the bleak economic and social circumstances surrounding young people at that time. It was enough to make you want to holler and throw up one's hands in disgust. Today's 21st century young males have a radically different perspective of family than the one embraced by past generations. The United States Census has many definitions of family. There is the blended family, the step family, the adopted family, the gay family, the single parent family, the grandparent led family and many others as we evolve and move further into the 21st century.

For many young men a family need not be blood kin. Our mobile society has forced many young men to gravitate to anyone that shows them some degree of compassion or someone who seems concerned about their well being. They often do not stop to think about the toxic, harmful relationships that can evolve out of these often times casual relationships.

"People without information cannot act responsibly. People with information are compelled to act responsibly."

—Author Unknown

The Innocence of A Time Gone By

By Charles Michael Choice

As I look back into time and freeze a frame
It's 1960, the splendor of serenity and peace

69

Neighborhoods busy with children playing
where everyone is aware of the season
when we knew the fruit trees were ripe
time to raid Mr. Walters' orchard, ah!
The sweetness of the cherries, plums, apples!
Two feet of fresh snow, gliding down that
steep hill, watch out for that big oak tree!
Playing little league baseball, proud to wear
that uniform displaying Precision Rubber!
Riding my Western Flyer with my best buds
to the far end of town, getting home by dark!
Delivering the morning newspaper to my 55
customers at 5 a. m. with an 8 dog escort!
Pushing that old lawnmower up and down the
street, I'll cut the front and back for $2.
Eating candied apples at the local carnival!
Just being so happy with life, a time gone by.
A slice of Americana, or just a glimpse of it all!

SIGNIFICANCE OF FAMILY

The absence of strong, stable families continues to have a profoundly negative impact on the lives of children. The fortunate children who grow up in families that provide the basic essentials of shelter, food, clothing and a firm guiding hand are being nurtured the same way that many Baby Boomers reminisce about. Our parents did the best that they could and were anything but perfect, and yet they understood their role and supplemented it with the support of uncles, grandparents, and cousins. The community and extended family had a personal stake and responsibility in the success of each child. Children of this generation held a great deal of respect and at times fear of these individuals. We courted favor with them! There was never any ambiguity about what grownups expected from the younger generation.

Retribution would be swift and complete whenever a child dared to get out of line in the presence of community leaders. These family and community "Elders" were the admired ladies and gentlemen of the time and were expected to be treated as such. This meant that regardless of whether or not there was a blood relationship, these people would take it upon themselves to correct and chastise misbehaving youth without impunity. It was an expectation of their esteemed position! There was an unwritten rule that the men were expected to take care of the women, children and their communities.

The positive code of conduct centered on discipline and respect was considered essential building blocks that all were expected to adhere to. These concepts were seared into each child's psyche at a very early age. Possessing good manners was a dominant expectation regardless of the educational attainment of your parents. You were expected to never embarrass your home or community. There was always a strong spiritual base within the community and there was little question about whether or not children would be actively involved in the church. Worship service often began with the early Sunday morning service and would sometimes continue nonstop throughout the entire day.

Education and school at that time were vastly different from what is currently in place. A school during that time was a way to begin to put those very vivid childhood, family, and community dreams of success into reality. Young men were expected to practice the life lessons handed down from the Community Elders and to strive for excellence at all times. There was little doubt of why children attended these schools. They were expected to follow the rules, stay out of trouble, and achieve academically. The teachers during this time period seemed more nurturing and yet more demanding. They refused to accept excuses from students for not getting assignments in on time or not doing your very best work at all times.

Teachers saw it as their duty, as Community Elders, to address these problems immediately and harshly at times! Teachers were in close contact with parents and guardians and often lived in the same community or even on the same street. There was a strong bond established between home and school. Young men seemed to know and understand their place in school and ultimately where they were going in life. This was a period of great optimism as opposed to the great despair that presently engulfs a large swath of America's children during the 21st century.

We can no longer allow the social malaise and abhorrent behavior surrounding America's young men to continue. We cannot allow our dispiriting present to become our permanently diminished future. Americans have too much history of accomplishments to simply give into this period of despair. Harold Melvin and the Blue Notes sang in one of their many hits, "Wake up everybody, no more sleeping in bed, no more backward thinking, it's time for thinking ahead."

Groups of concerned Black, White, and Latino citizens must generate solutions to these problems. Any person can mentor a child. It only takes a willingness to serve. Teachers, counselors, coaches and administrators must take up the mantle of hope and design programs that capture the interest of America's boys at an early age. Mentoring groups must redouble their efforts to save American boys from themselves.

We must be proactive and develop practical solutions that they find palatable. We must use our places of worship to help provide home training lessons for young men. We must teach them how to talk to other adults and children without swearing and otherwise being incoherent. In addition, we can sponsor dress-for-success seminars so that young men can become acquainted with suits, shirts and ties. They must understand that the wing-tip shoe or the penny loafer can replace Timberland boots.

Fraternities, sororities and social clubs must become much more involved if we are to save this next generation. In some ways we must meet them on their own terms. Music is a compelling force in the lives of the young. Let us sponsor some contests that also have life lessons attached to them. As adults, we have to also think about our own self interests. Many of us cannot retire because of the young men and women that we see each day acting irresponsibly. The exterior problem of sagging pants serves as a powerful metaphor for a much bigger, more substantive problem: turning hopelessness into hope. We must collectively speak up and speak out and help redirect America's young men to believe that they control their own fate and destiny.

Families must be there to support all young people but, especially young men, during their transition years. There are new ideas and theories being developed every day. Some seem worthy of exploration. Some researchers have noted that church attendance has as much effect on a teen's grade point average GPA as whether the teen's parents earned a college degree. Students in grades 7-12 who went to church weekly also had lower dropout rates and felt more of a connection to their schools. The study listed several reasons why students could be performing better. Church attendance provides consistent contact with positive adults who may serve as role models. Regular church attendance provides parents a forum to communicate with other parents who have similar beliefs. Friendships develop between students who have similar values and who are more likely to participate in extracurricular activities.

There are those who strongly suggest that parents should have their kids attend places of worship and they believe that religious participation has a positive effect on academics. This research may be food for thought for those parents who are not interested in attending church can consider how to structure their kids' time to allow access to the same beneficial social networks and opportunities religious institutions provide.

This exciting new research notes that individuals and families benefit from social networking as well as the psychological benefits of church attendance. Children who attend church on a regular basis are more likely to have friends who genuinely care about doing the right thing and higher academic attainment such as GPAs (grade point averages). In conclusion, the importance of religion to teens had very little impact on their educational outcomes. That suggests that the act of attending the social and structural parts of church could be more important to educational outcomes than the religion itself. This research was consistent across all denominations.

CONNECTING TO A POSITIVE FAMILY

I recently read a compelling book that recounted the life of three very at risk young men growing up in urban New York City who eventually became doctors. These three young men grew up in households that were devoid of strong fathers. Their heroes were not the current men in their young lives. It was as though many men in their lives were incidental or unimportant to them. They even believed and aspired to not grow up to be like their biological fathers. These three friends outlined their plan for supporting each other and dared to dream big and to also hold each other accountable as they continued to evolve into young men.

In an age when positive male role models were and continue to be so important, these young men, with the assistance of their mothers and grand-mothers, negotiated the many trails and tribulations of life by working in concert with each other. They did not let the overwhelming odds against their success diminish their high ideals and goals. The women in their lives were left to raise and transform these boys into responsible young men. These women left little doubt about the basic core values they would demand of their sons. They insisted that their sons obtain a quality education and to not be seduced by the temptations of street life.

The absence of strong fathers left great voids in their personal lives and yet these three young men were able to overcome the almost daily challenges by uniting and maintaining the high standards set in each of their individual households. These beliefs encouraged them to only hang out with people who had similar progressive ideas about life and growing into responsible men. Many times they had to see what not to do in order to better understand what to do! The importance of education was the cornerstone of their vision for success. They would become obsessed with achieving this goal. They readily acknowledge that it would have been nice to have strong dads in their lives but, they were dealt a different hand. Through sheer perseverance and determination they are now considered role models for legions of young men to follow in the future.

This book was written to share valuable knowledge to others who may experience the challenges of growing themselves into viable, responsible 21st century husbands, fathers, and community leaders. The young men in this book

all agreed that obtaining a quality education will even up the playing field of
life because it is the great equalizer when all things are said and done. The
young men in this book understood that you cannot tackle the many complex
issues alone while growing up. They subscribed to the "Buddy System" and its
importance of developing a close network of friends who have similar beliefs.
They encourage young men to get involved in their community and to always
give back more than you take from it. They all strongly advocated volunteer-
ism. They were convinced that you will be richly rewarded by helping others.

Finally, these young men believed that it was important to secure a responsible male mentor at a very early age because of the need to have someone
with wisdom to serve as a sounding board for new ideas and experiences.
All three young men stressed the significance of valuing and respecting all
women contrary to what the latest music videos may suggest. They strongly
believed that young men should strive to eliminate unproductive, idle times
in their lives by keeping their eyes on the prize.

FAMILY LIFE'S IMPACTS ON
SCHOOL ACHIEVEMENT

Author, Reginald M. Clark, "Family Life and School Achievement: Why Poor
Black Children Succeed or Fail" offered an array of sound advice that all parents
must be aware of. The following Reginald M. Clark chart provides a valuable tool
that can be used to determine whether or not one is providing the kind of adult led
nurturing environment that allows children to flourish in school settings.

The seventeen patterns serve to distinguish the family success orientation.
Many Americans acknowledge that these family psychosocial patterns are
basic to literacy acquisition. Further research is needed to determine the
relative weight of the pattern categories overall, and for various ethnic,
socioeconomic, and gender groups. It is possible that sets (or clusters)
of significant patterns may emerge from among the seventeen we have
identified (e.g., parents' expectations and action patterns). For example,
parents may have had high expectations for some students who are not high
achievers. That is, they wanted their children to achieve, but did not know
how to bring it about.

Reginald M. Clark's has created a very important chart that should be
indelibly etched into the mindset of each 21st century parent who hopes and
expects student academic success in America's public schools. These are the
new standard school rules of engagement that should be adhered to by parents
and family members who have high academic expectations for their children.
Strong family ties are essential to the success of 21st Century young men.

Table 4.1. Reginald M. Clark's A Comparison of the Quality of Success-Producing Patterns in Homes of High Achievers and Low Achievers

High Achievers	Low Achievers
1. Frequent school contact initiated by by parent	Infrequent school contact initiated parent
2. Child has had some stimulating supportive school teachers	Child has no stimulating supportive school teachers
3. Parents psychologically and emotionally calm with child centered	Parents in psychological and emotional upheaval with child
4. Students psychologically and emotionally calm with parents	Students less psychologically and emotionally calm with parents
5. Parents expect to play major role in child's schooling	Parents have lower expectations of playing role in child's schooling
6. Parents expect child to play major role in child's schooling	Parents have lower expectation of child's role in child's schooling
7. Parents expect child to get post-secondary training	Parents have lower expectation that child will get postsecondary training
8. Parents have explicit achievement centered rules and norms	Parents have less explicit achievement rules and norms
9. Students show long-term acceptance of norms as legitimate	Students have less long-term acceptance of norms
10. Parents establish clear, specific role boundaries and status structures with parents as dominant authority	Parents establish more blurred boundaries and status structures
11. Siblings interact as organized subgroups	Siblings are a less structured, interactive subgroups
12. Conflict between family members is infrequent	Conflict between some family members is frequent
13. Parents frequently engage in deliberate achievement training activities	Parents seldom engage in deliberate achievement training activities
14. Parents frequently engage in implicit achievement training activities	Parents engage less frequently in implicit achievement training
15. Parents exercise firm, consistent monitoring and rules enforcement	Parents have inconsistent standards and exercise less monitoring of child's time and space
16. Parents provide liberal nurturance and support	Parents are less liberal with nurturance and support
17. Parents defer to child's knowledge in intellectual matters	Parents do not defer to child in intellectual matters

Now is not the time to abandon young men or to leave life changing decisions to the emotions of immature young adults. The odds of success for young men have been altered significantly against them. One should begin new, healthy family traditions that are more inclusive and supportive. Family does not necessarily mean a nuclear mother, father, and children. It is time for us to breathe new life into that old mantra "It takes a Village to raise a child."

A good example is the family gathering that takes place in my home each year. My wife (Sarah) and I have hosted our extended family's Thanksgiving Day Celebration for the past twenty years. It is attended by over 50 relatives and friends who look forward to coming together to share fellowship, food, and to catch up on what has been taking place over the past year. This event has proven to be an excellent way to reconnect and to bask in family accomplishments and hear some of life's challenges for individuals. This is also the time to find creative ways to support anyone who is in need of networking advice or special prayer.

The family must play an ever expanding role in the lives of 21st century males if, for no other reason than to provide a strong alternative to the lure of gangs. Gang membership across America has grown exponentially based on its mission of providing a different kind of family that cares about them unconditionally and provides someone who will always have their back.

Chapter 5

Parenting 21st Century Males

In 1971, Marvin Gaye penned the song "What's Going On." These heart wrenching lyrics described the anguish on the part of 20th century parents raising children during those very turbulent and complicated times. He eloquently highlighted the despair and ambiguity that engulfed and consumed the lives of parents while attempting to raise their children a generation ago. Today's parents must stop being reactive and become much more proactive.

Parents must be responsible for raising their own offspring and not be overly dependent on the educational system to do the job for them. Parents must begin child rearing with the end in mind. What is it that you want to see your son become? Parents need to stop pampering and smothering their boys and begin to invest time and energy into their social, emotional, and physical development. Why have so many parents given up and abdicated their right to determine the future of their sons?

Do you know of programs and individuals out there who can help to enhance your son's life experiences? What are your realistic expectations for your child? Children will rise or fall to the levels of expectations that are set by adults they trust. Parents need to stop letting strangers determine the fate of their children! These notions whether factually true or not provide a glimpse into the hopelessness and frustrations of large groups of parents. It echoes the perceptions of large ethnic groups whether real or not.

The "Mean Moms" poem discusses a message that needs to be shared with our sons. This poem talks about how demanding this child's mother was while growing up. It shares some personal thoughts on motherly behaviors and expectations and how unreasonable they are about even the smallest things such as what could be eaten at breakfast. This student described being upset with this mother for not being allowed to eat fast foods whenever there was an urge. The mother instead, insisted that a fully balanced breakfast, lunch or dinner be consumed at each meal. This poem also shared how unreasonable it was for the mother to insist on knowing the whereabouts of her children at all times. This mean mother wanted to know about the friends her children hung out with and even wanted to know more about their parents.

This poem discussed the mean mother's adherence to forced labor and how the child was made to do chores in the home on a regular basis. The mean mom poem is summed up by the child reflecting on the terrible childhood that was endured but, grudgingly acknowledging that the world needs more mean moms. Successfully raising 21st century children is very difficult and yet parents are expected to guide their offspring onward and upward in spite of the many obstacles that life will place in your pathway. The demanding parent is just one way of accomplishing this very important task!

WHAT BOYS NEED

Protecting the emotional life of boys should be a very high priority for parents who have the responsibility of raising boys to grow up in healthy productive environments. We need to produce many more emotionally grounded males in the world today. Young men need to become more empathetic and knowledgeable about the type of man they desire to become. It is never too early to plant the seeds of excellence in everything they do. Far too many 21st century young men are seen as devoid of anything remotely connected with feelings and compassion.

America must eliminate this distorted view that does not acknowledge a boy's capacity to show any kind of concern for others. We must hold young men to the same high cultural standards that have been demanded of generations past. Increased expectations in boys such as self control, emotional honesty, and moral responsibility should be emphasized at an early age.

The old excuse of "Boys Will Be Boys" must no longer be tolerated and must be eliminated once and for all if responsible adults are to consistently help young men grow emotionally well balanced. American schools must provide support and guidance that make sense to a young man's unique DNA. 21st century young men must better harness their emotional responses if they are to become the productive sons, husbands and citizens America desperately needs. Our nation's high standard of excellence is at stake if we fail to correct this challenge.

Research suggests a variety of ways to nurture the emotional life of boys. American parents must help boys develop an emotional vocabulary that is often very foreign to males. Young men must be able to understand themselves before we can expect them to successfully interact and communicate with adults and other young people. The following observations should be noted when developing the emotional intelligence of boys:

1. Boys are engaged and very active by nature
2. Boys have their own masculine language of communication that we must validate
3. Courage and empathy are signs of strength in men, not weaknesses
4. Self discipline is essential for building character and a sense of consciousness.
5. Manhood is modeled through emotional attachment not isolation
6. There is no single model for being a responsible male, the list is endless

In the past, there were reasons for entire communities to internalize and celebrate measures of achievement. Athletic celebrations were just one of the examples. For African American parents, the success of any one black person in any new field was perceived as a vicarious victory for the entire black community because that individual was opening doors that had at one time been closed to blacks. Younger blacks could then emulate the example of the pioneer and follow in their footsteps. This ultimately led to the community as a whole pulling itself out of the conditions that were the legacy of slavery.

The 21st century has seen the dawn of a new uneasy consciousness that is not necessarily in the best interest of a healthy intellectual growth of the at large community. Group identity and psychology which researchers have investigated for generations are somewhat different in today's hectic world. Researchers discovered that young black people during the 1960s, followed Malcolm X's lead and saw things radically differently from the establishment. These young people believed that the success of ethnic pioneers did not result in widespread success. They felt that a few more blacks made it into the professions, but nowhere near the numbers necessary to lift up the whole community. The personal strategy for the success of the community had changed dramatically.

This new attitude reasoned that the strategy of using individual success to lead to community success was fatally flawed. This became an alternative strategy to be strongly considered for those living during this time frame. The new theory believed that the only way that the majority of the black community could advance was if all its members stick together and advance in lock step. This led to the conviction that any attempt by individuals to pursue academic success would be seen as an act of opposition to their race. There were no exceptions to this rule! Individuals who excelled academically were expected to conform to the new norms of acceptable black behavior. This belief system ensured that this form of ethnic identity would remain intact.

This world view has created significant problems for those black students who have higher academic aspirations. These students are torn between wanting to achieve academic success because of their parents' expectations and their desire to stay on good terms and in step with their peers in order to retain important adolescent relationships. A growing number of these students subscribed to a middle of the road approach that keeps grades just high enough to avoid conflict at home while preserving friendships at school and staying on the good side of teachers.

Much research has been generated in recent years about the relationship between effort and reward when it comes to academic performance. It is generally thought that people are more likely to work harder if they can see a benefit in the return and have a realistic expectation of receiving that benefit. There are many professionals who embrace the theory that educational effort leads to academic credentials, which will result in gainful employment. There are those who believe that black students underachieve because of their often mass rejection of the effort/reward concept which forms the basis of the white work ethic.

The effort/reward relationship is not always obvious to black students. This may be the result of a long history of being denied employment and education commensurate with their efforts. Higher levels of education and employment were consistently denied to blacks solely because of their race or ethnicity regardless of how much they valued education. Many researchers conclude that this was a major reason for blacks to not see the work/credential/ employment as applying to them, as their white counterparts do.

Many mothers today raise their daughters and love their sons. It is far too common that some mothers have low expectations for academic excellence and seldom assign household chores to their sons. Girls are expected to perform well in school as well as share housework responsibilities. Many 21st century parents emphasize the stereotype that household chores and academics are only for girls. This philosophy creates conflicting expectations in adult male-female relationships. There are many rites of passage developments and other important learning experiences that positively and negatively affect young American males. These are things that older experienced males take for granted that are often seen as a mystery to boys growing up under the guidance of single parent women.

A child's quality of life is determined more than just by race, class, or gender. The relationship between mothers and their sons has become an increasingly complex issue as we move further into the 21st century. Many people equate differences with deficiencies. There is no doubt that a number of Black people think differently from whites. There are those who conclude that this difference is evidence of white superiority. There is little question that black and white students respond and see things differently from one another. It is the responsibility of all teachers to develop strategies to maximize the potential of each student.

Identifying Male Defiance

Many males look at their teachers and are immediately labeled as defiant which oftentimes leads to what has been described as a showdown between the female teacher and the boy. Teachers are not always able to use their previous advantage of size to discipline them as boys grow taller. The conflict will not always match strength against strength. Some female teachers are afraid of young men. Professionals cannot effectively teach any child that they fear. This negative relationship with the teacher leads some boys to become the class clown to mask their academic deficiencies. Their following negative behavior illustrates signs of a bad relationship with the teacher:

1. Ignoring teacher instructions
2. Concentrating on non-academic discussions
3. Wearing headphones and listening to music
4. Reading magazines and other literature not related to the class
5. Using inappropriate humor
6. Responding sarcastically to others
7. Throwing things such as paper and other items
8. Bringing technology into the classroom for personal reasons
9. Cheating and cutting corners on exams and assignments
10. Dozing off or sleeping in class

Emotional protection begins when parents love, care and touch their boys. It is also very important to say civil thing to children. We must affirm the positive things that boys do and not highlight the negative. Do we affirm each other, or are we constantly negating each other? We must approach each other in a civil manner and have substantive conversations with our children, with our spouse, with our friends and with our colleagues. Emotional protection takes place when we successfully interact with our boys and how we behave at home.

We need to regularly discuss at dinner time the things that are important to the future success of our sons. Americans need to talk about how children should behave when away from home. Americans need to examine and then put into place systems necessary to ensure that all children will not have so many debilitating transitions to make in isolation. These transitions can be very paralyzing if a child has to suffer through them without first having meaningful discussion in the home.

PROTECTING YOUR TEENS

Boys will be boys and girls will be girls, but they are still kids. In the midst of many kinds of change, these kids are searching for their identities and a sense of autonomy. They are often ultra sensitive to criticism. They have a great need to be independent. They need to see where they fit in. They are more likely to look to peers for guidance than to parents. They may challenge adult values and choose their own way of doing things, even though they will be guided through it all by what they have been taught while living at home. Teenagers often behave irrationally when in the general public. This results in many adults choosing not to stand up to those teens who challenge them. In many poor communities, teenagers are at real risk of not getting through this stage safely.

Young men will need our help if they are to move on to a productive and successful adulthood. We must stay committed and involved to assist them on their quest to make sense during this difficult period of their life. There are many challenges that may confront them such as dropping out of school, getting pregnant, getting shot, stealing from others, shooting up, getting drunk, getting high, and going to jail, catching AIDS or STDs, killing themselves intentionally or otherwise. Adults must help provide a safe harbor for them. Concerned adults should reach out and provide structure and support whether you are a parent, a caregiver, a relative or a friend.

The 19th century French naturalist Jean-Henri Fabre conducted experiments with caterpillars because they had a tendency to march in unison. He would place them around a flower pot and then watched as they marched in a circle day after day. The scientist then introduced food (pine needles) into the equation in the center of the pot just to see how the caterpillars would respond. They continued to walk in unison around the outer edge of the pot until one by one they died of starvation just inches from a life sustaining food source.

These caterpillars in many ways are comparable to 21st century mothers. These mothers seem to be marching in unison around the proverbial flower pot of life from sun up to sun down. They hold important jobs outside the house. They are still responsible for raising, feeding, chauffeuring, house cleaning, family relationships, and the spiritual development of their children. Some experts conclude that this overcommitted and breathless pace of life is self destructive for parents in many of today's Western nations. The analogy can be made that mothers must break the current physically demanding child rearing habits or run the risk of ending up like the caterpillars in naturalist Jean Henri-Fabre experiments. This uninterrupted pattern has mothers forever wondering how they will be able to get things done day after day.

Mothers must immediately break this exhaustive, unproductive cycle if they are to raise healthy, intellectually curious young men, while, at the same time salvaging their own personal well being. We do not have the luxury of raising our child all over again. It is counterproductive to point fingers and blame others. We need to connect now while we have the opportunity. We need to value the time we spend with our boys and learn as much about their personal likes and dislikes as possible. We must be firm as well as affirm. We must model the behavior we want to see young men exhibit at all times.

WOMEN AND MALE DISCONNECT

There have been extensive researches on the connection between boys, mothers, and women. A mother's connection to her son becomes strained as a boy grows into manhood. There will come a point when a young boy must shift his attention from his mother to his father. This does not mean that the mother and son should abandon or write off one another. The mother-son relationship will go through a transformation and the boy will seem to reject the close bonds that were developed between the two. This would be problematic if the intent is for the successful transitioning of young men into responsible adults.

Young boys cannot and should not abandon those humanistic concepts that mothers embody such as love, intimacy, and warmth. Mothers continuously face the new dilemma of whether or not the time is right to let her son go. Many mothers want to preserve that closeness, but they do not know how. Many women fear losing their much loved sons and yet they feel compelled to cut the apron strings. A mother who cares about her son and wants what is best for him can easily fall victim to this challenge.

Mothers must decide whether staying too close to her son will turn him into a sissy or mama's boy. A boy will increasingly demonstrate his need to feel independent, capable, and uniquely male. A mother generally provides love and acceptance to her son but boys will sometimes distance himself from her when he feels the urge to reassert his autonomy. This is a natural response and yet a boy never loses his need to be understood and loved by his mother.

This constant tug of war between independence and a deep need to hold on often confuses many mothers. The boy's most significant mission is to grow up and adapt to the challenge of becoming a young man. The mother's most important mission is to guide and nurture their son in ways that are often seen as unmanly. There will be natural conflicts between the goals of mothers and boys as they continue to mature. These phenomena will continue to be a conflict that will not be easily resolved as the young man ages.

ANGER AND VIOLENCE

As a building principal, teacher, father, and conference lecturer, it is not uncommon for this author to interact with educators, parents, and community leaders who are perplexed by the growing anger within many of America's boys. Adults have no definitive answers to this challenge other than to become more effective listeners. When is the last time you sat down to give your undivided attention to a young man? How do we dissipate and redirect their avalanche of negative energy? There are many angry boys in public schools. Some of them we see in therapy, sent by teachers or parents concerned about their aggressive behavior or about underlying themes of anger or violence in their school writings. We also hear a lot about angry boys from their victims. We see other angry boys who evolve into the young bully who torments other children.

We see the silent brooding boy who looks like a powder keg ready to blow at the slightest provocation. The most powerful expression of anger is violence and we see a steady stream of that in the news every day. There is now a category when evaluating No Child Left Behind systems called 'The Most Dangerous Schools'. It is not surprising that this statistic is prominent when determining the effectiveness of school building sites. There are few images more heartbreaking than those of the recent past involving boys who shot, strangled, stabbed, or in some other way inflicted violence on others, including children, teachers, and their own parents.

What makes a child want to lash out and hurt others? There are many assumptions about this theory. Many experts note the dramatic rise in violence seen by children on television and movie screens. There are others who point to the glorification of violence in the popular culture, easy access to guns, growing up in an economically disadvantaged violent neighborhood, and more hours of reduced supervision brought about by the disappearance of the two parent family.

Some educational experts conclude that many boys' academic shame becomes anger, and that anger moves very rapidly to violence. Boys need support and emotional resources to deal with the loss of self esteem that they experience from a teacher's criticism, a parent's harsh comment, a classmate's taunt, or a girl's rejection. Parents, teachers and the at large community are challenged to teach the lessons of emotional intelligence that allows a boy to bend under emotional trials without breaking into violent revenge.

"Life isn't always fair. Learn to deal with it. You can't just go around hurting people every time you get angry. You need to consider how your actions affect others. Don't see threats where they don't exist. You need to know that controlling your anger does not make you a sissy."

—Author Unknown

DISCIPLINING BOYS

It is very important for boys to understand the significance of authority. It is also important for parents to avoid the extremes that range from oppressiveness and rigidity to being overly permissive. There should be some balance because the overreliance of one of these strategies could be damaging to any child. Centuries ago it was common to note that children were expected to be seen but, not heard. Fathers were seen as dictatorial, and the enforcers of the family. Children were known to fear if not respect their dads. It was important for parents to physically whip children into shape in preparing them to become normally functioning adults.

The role of mothers was to provide nurturance but, they could be strict and punitive when the need occurred. This tough love type of upbringing is something many baby boomers experienced. The child rearing pendulum swung to the opposite end during the 1960s through the 1990s where an emphasis was placed on the child centered approach. This approach diminished strict authority and created an oftentimes unstable environment for young people living at home. Many children were taught to question anything and everything and to value very little about the world they lived in at that time. This challenge is at the heart of America's challenge in reconnecting with our boys.

Chapter 6

Public Schools Evolving From Teachers to Academic Coaches

The thought provoking lyrics of "Wake Up Everybody" written in 1975, by singer Teddy Pendergrass makes a statement about the dramatic changes that must take place in public schools across 21st century America. We have experienced significant changes in the world and yet we continue to rely on tired old practices in our school houses. Students and parents are demanding a brand new way of teaching if we expect the world to get better. It is unconscionable to continue to accept the dismal outcome of far too many schools in America's once proud public educational system without a dramatic overhaul. We know that today's 21st century students want to be inspired by well informed, well trained, and well intentioned educators. The following poem says a great deal about the importance of good teaching.

Love Being a Teacher
The Mediocre Teacher Will Only Give Directions
The Good Teacher Provides Further Clarification
The Superior Teacher Paints A Vivid Picture
The Great Teacher Inspires A Call For Individual Action!

A TIME TO INSPIRE

We need capable, caring teachers who understand the importance of nurturing dreams. They must be able to do all of the following:

1. To replenish
2. To renew

3. To re energize
4. To restore
5. To rekindle
6. To rehabilitate and
7. To recommit to the precious young people we have been entrusted to help grow and nurture.

There is a heightened need for educators to make dramatic changes in their approach with students. That change has little to do with the purchase of new equipment and new electronic devices. Good teachers have long realized that developing a positive relationship with students goes a long way in determining the amount and breadth of learning that takes place in classrooms and schools. American public education has overly relied on focusing its resources and talents on attempts to raise test scores and school improvement for the past thirty years with very inconsistent results.

Educational researchers have unveiled and implemented untold new teaching and learning strategies with little to show for it! Many experts believe that the most significant challenge before any 21st century educator is to develop a bond and a healthy working relationship between student and teacher.

There are many researchers who promote the creation of an emotional bank account to convey the crucial aspects of relationship building. One makes deposits and withdrawals in all relationships. The following lists are examples of deposits and withdrawals that are extremely important to young people:

The American family has been extensively studied for the past fifty years. The studies have centered on the youth, home, church, schools, peers, and the impact of television. The 1950s decade is often seen as a base to compare other periods because there were clear rules and schedules to adhere to. Families consisted of a father, mother, and children. Most families sat down

Deposits	Withdrawals
Seek first to understand	Seek first to be understood
Keeping promises	Your word is not valued
Promote kindness, courtesies	Universally rude/no empathy
Clarifying expectations	Being deliberately ambiguous
Loyalty to the absent	Not trustworthy
Apologies	Do not accept any blame for failures
Being open to feedback	Not receptive to criticism

for dinner to enjoy conversations at the table revolved around each family member's experience during that day.

The home and family was the major influence on a child. The second major influence on children of the 1950s was church. School was the third major influence on children's lives during this period. Peers came in fourth on the list of influences was followed by the impact of television. This information should serve as a reference point for adults when working with today's youth. If anyone should care about students, it should be home and family. When children are let down over a consistent period of time by home and family, it becomes difficult to believe anyone else really cares about them or their well-being.

It is oftentimes confusing to a child when someone outside that home and family demonstrates interest in them. Once you earn their trust, what do you have to do to keep it? Adults must learn to be honest when interacting with children. Children will instantly end any relationship for good with adults if they feel you are being less than forthcoming with them. Children are resilient and can handle the truth. Children have little tolerance for lies and liars.

Teachers can gain the trust of challenging students by spending additional time with those students outside of school. Some of the most effective way is to attend their athletic events, proms or awards banquets. We must illustrate that we care by showing up on our own personal time and staying for the entire event because action speaks much louder then words. It has been proven that children respond more strongly to the nonverbal cues than to all the words in the world. It sends a powerful message to children to see their teachers spending their personal time outside of school to witness their activities.

The message of care is transmitted well beyond the walls of the classroom. Teachers must understand that they need to connect with both their good and bad students. This will translates into enormous teacher power! It is establishing this relationship with difficult students that underscores a teacher's true character and demonstrates a teacher's willingness to go the extra mile for all students.

Educators must be cognizant of how we interact with our students on a daily basis. How do we approach them? What do we say to them? How do we say it? What about our body language? Are we diminishing without even opening our mouths through nonverbal communications? Each of these actions can negatively affect our students and our ability to teach them well. A teacher must personally connect with each student before he or she can teach that student. The 21st century student must believe that the teacher standing in front of them is approachable and has their best interest at heart.

WHAT SUCCESSFUL SCHOOLS LOOK LIKE

The Characteristics of Successful schools and school systems:

1. They all have a common vision and mission and everyone who works in or with the school knows what it is.
2. They all have quality leaders.
3. Students come first.
4. They have a quality professional development plan which the teacher/staff have helped to design.
5. Continuous improvement is a common thread.
6. There are positive relationships as well as encouragement and support.
7. There is a synergy to accomplish team goals by coming together as one entity with one mission.
8. There must be positive parental involvement/support.
9. Everyone understands their roles, from administrators, teachers, and support staff to students.
10. Failure is not an option.

"Nobody Rises to Low Expectations."

—Author Unknown

"I think about teachers who never accepted failure. Who, when you had finished a school year and moved on to the next grade, you automatically knew who your last teacher was? They seemed to put their stamp on you."

—Author Unknown

IN SUPPORT OF NURTURE

In looking at the causes of individual differences in intelligence, a major issue is the relative contribution of genetics and environment. The intellectual and cultural "flavor" of a time and place (the zeitgeist) has swung back and forth over time with regard to the amount of influence that nature vs. nurture has on human intelligence. In the late 1800's, as Darwinism took off, the role of genetically determined capability was considered very important. This was in contrast, for example, to the 1960's, in the USA, when views were more in favor of a "tabula rasa" (blank slate) view of human intelligence. They believed that people are capable of much more, if given enriching environmental conditions in which to reach their potential.

The term tabula rasa (blank slate in Latin) refers to the epistemological thesis that individual human beings are born with no innate or built in mental content. They believed that a person's entire resource of knowledge is built up gradually from their experiences and sensor perceptions of the outside world. Proponents of the tabula rasa thesis favor the "nurture" side of the nature versus nurture debate, when it comes to aspects of one's personality, social and emotional behavior, and intelligence.

The Zeitgeist in the Western psychological world is somewhere in between. Both genetics and environment are seen as playing important roles in the development of children. The modern view about nature vs. nurture in intelligence is interaction oriented. Some researchers note that Mother Nature has not entrusted the determination of our intellectual capacities to the blind fate of a gene or genes. Mother Nature gave us parents, learning, language, culture and education to program ourselves. The focus of the problem shifted in the 1960s, away from the individual as the cause of the problem, and centered on social determinants.

The pendulum swung towards the nurture/environment end and away from the nature/genetic end. Efforts were made to address poor educational achievement through quality public schooling. Some researchers strongly suggested that given twelve randomly selected healthy infants would lead to twelve well adjusted professionals when they interacted with well trained skillful individuals. This meant that students had great opportunities to become doctors, lawyers, artists, merchants, chefs regardless of his talents, penchants, tendencies, abilities, vocations, and race of his ancestors.

This is an area of research that is still evolving. The nature vs. nurture debate has raged along with the contribution of interactions between genetics and environment on IQ variance. In the focus on nature vs. nurture issues, the attempts to estimate the relative contribution rests on the somewhat naïve notion that there is a constant, true value. Gene expression is environmentally dependent and it is impossible to obtain pure estimates of genetic vs. environmental contributions one could not exist without the other.

The environment a child experiences is partly a consequence of the child's genes as well as external factors. A person seeks out and creates his or her environment. If the child is of a mechanical interest that child practices mechanical skills: if a bookworm that child seeks out books. Genes may create an appetite rather than an aptitude. A future area for research which blends those in the nature camps with those in the nurture camps would be to examine which environmental components allow people to optimally realize their genetic potential for a variety of areas of cognitive performance.

There are a number of factors about the transmission of intelligence that virtually everyone seems to accept:

1. Both heredity and environment contribute to intelligence.
2. Heredity and environment interact in various ways.
3. Extremely poor as well as highly enriched environments can interfere with the realization of a person's intelligence, regardless of the person's heredity
4. Although most would accept a causal role of genetics, the exact genetic link and how it operates is far from being understood. It is not a single gene, but a complex combination of smaller genetic markers.
5. It is difficult to pin-down single, identifiable elements of the environment which directly influence IQ scores. Several factors appear to influence intelligence.

There is extensive debate regarding this notion of students entering 21st century schools with overwhelming learning deficits. One must now consider that each student, no matter how impoverished, no matter how great the language barrier, no matter how dysfunctional their current family, comes to school with a personal culture that needs to be acknowledged and affirmed. These children have personal value to bring to America's middle class public school philosophy. We need to work with the experiences that these students bring to our schools and classrooms and not be so eager to marginalize their individual frame of references. Most students, in many instances, bring a rich heritage that educators need to build upon and not be so hasty to decry as inferior and not worth salvaging.

There needs to be much more in depth discussion regarding the intellectual gifts and talents children brings to public schools. There are those who feel that the child either has academic potential or does not! The intelligence quotient declines over time in children raised in deprived environments, such as circumstances of poverty and isolation. IQ improves in children who leave deprived environments and enter enriched environments. One must simply reference back to successful coaching models to gain some insight on the importance of nurturing and motivating today's young people.

Most capable athletic coaches start with the players that are in front of them. They take the existing talent and build that group of individuals into the well drilled team that always competes for a championship even when their talent level says that they should not. Unfortunately, this is almost polar opposite of what actually takes place in far too many of America's public school classrooms. Many teachers take a glance at the students seated before them in their classroom and almost immediately declare that there is not much intellectual talent evident this school year.

These same teachers then go on to live out that 'Self Fulfilling Prophecy.' There has been much scientific research regarding teacher expectation research. There is little question that high academic expectations for all students should be the mantra for America's 21st century public schools.

HOW TO CREATE MORE GOOD SCHOOLS

1. Extend positive school experiences beyond the school day
2. Introduce early intervention programs
3. Develop mentor–student relationships
4. Broaden the definition of intelligence
5. Respect for all learners
6. Encourage students to explore their gifts instead of dwelling on their deficiencies

A teacher's relationship with boys can be essential in building a boy's resilience and connection to their work in schools. Specifically, we must examine how teachers understand the ways that their relationships with boys shape their teaching practice as well as their understandings of boys' learning in school. As boys achievement continues to fall behind, we must engage the question of how teachers come to know the boys they teach. How can we better communicate with 21st century boys? How can we get them to better transition into the successful academic life within our classroom and our schools? This author suggests that one should look no further than a thorough analysis of a school's athletic teams to gain more insight into the young male psyche.

Sports are second only to religion as the most powerful cultural force in American Society. It provides our youth with several ways to develop:

1. It provides fun and instant gratification
2. It fulfills a need for friendship and a sense of belonging to an organization
3. It offers an opportunity for healthier minds and bodies through physical exercise
4. It offers longer term cumulative benefits through hard work and the power to dream.
5. It affirms the relationship between hard work and positive recognition.

SPORTS METAPHORS

Metaphors are figures of speech in which a word or phrase literally denoting one kind of objective idea is used in place of another to suggest a likeness or analogy between them. The language of sports is very important to males in general but, young males in particular. You either know the language as an insider or as an outsider. When examining football, sports pages don't just report the facts. There is a lot more information that is embedded in the story that you must have a personal understanding before fully grasping the unwritten meanings. Most people generally know the final score. Males get turned on by the vivid language that engages the reader on an emotional level.

A metaphor is a figure of speech that compares two different things without using a word of comparison such as "like or as." A good example is to write a noun that relates to a sport such as baseball, basketball, football, soccer, or hockey. Now think of something to compare it to. Write your metaphor. An example would be the baseball bat was a branch swishing at the ball. Baseball bat and branch are compared to each other. The following information can be utilized to begin to understand the significance and relevancy of sports metaphors.

Activity 6.1.   Popular Sports Metaphors

Home Run	Being # 1
Grand Slam	Stay in the Game
Setbacks & Sacks	Keep your nose to the grindstone
Double Play	Teamwork
Slam Dunk	Don't let your team Down
Hole in One	Stepping up to the Plate
Run Interference	Down the Stretch
Measuring Up	

These sports terms have a special meaning to most young males and yet they are rarely mentioned in our academic classrooms. The increased use of metaphors is nothing more than a reestablishing of lines of communications between teachers and students. How could you use five of these metaphors in your classroom or school? There are very significant issues that need to be explored as we closely examine why a particular school can be so successful in athletics and yet a dismal failure in academics? We see this widespread phenomenon in school after school all across America.

Why is it that the same athletes that turned out to be exceptional on the playing field can find little success in the classroom? Boys were celebrated as scholar- athletes not too many years ago. Today's males self-categorize themselves as either scholars or as athletes/jocks. Are things so radically different in our classrooms that unless you are deemed academically talented, boys do not have the proclivity to be successful in America's schools?

Fill in the following five charts to determine if your school is providing an academically nurturing environment for male students.

A COMPARISON OF ATHLETIC AND ACADEMIC PRACTICES

1. Students compete regularly and love competition
2. Students develop a "Strong Work Ethic" and enjoy preparing all week
3. Students are offered encouragement to improve continuously
4. Students know that mental and physical discipline is important
5. Student morale is positive and essential
6. Students look and feel like they belong.
   Your Comparison

Table 6.1.   A Comparison of Athletic and Academic Practices

Athletic Coaches	Academic Teachers	
		Question #1
		Question #2
		Question #3
		Question #4
		Question #5
		Question #6

7. Students learn valuable lessons even in defeat.
8. Students learn to adjust and accept constructive criticism as a natural part of improvement.
9. Students do not give up in the face of insurmountable odds
10. Students know that success depends on good communication skills
11. Students know that they have an important role in the success of the whole group
12. Students know that "Tough Love" is sometimes necessary and that adults care enough about them to sometimes correct them.
    Your Comparison

Table 6.2.   A Comparison of Athletic and Academic Practices

Athletic Coaches	Academic Teachers	
		Question #7
		Question #8
		Question #9
		Question #10
		Question #11
		Question #12

13. Students make a commitment to finish what they start
14. Students know that when mistakes are pointed out to them it is their responsibility to improve and to get better
15. Students know that change is continuous and fluid
16. Students know that they can control their own destiny and future
17. Students are not overly sensitive about criticism
18. Students do not blame others when things break down and do not go well
    Your Comparison

Table 6.3   A Comparison of Athletic and Academic Practices

Athletic Coaches	Academic Teachers	
		Question #13
		Question #14
		Question #15
		Question #16
		Question #17
		Question #18

19. Students readily identify with the organizational purpose and understand their individual roles
20. Students know the rules and eagerly follow them
21. Students trust and have developed a close working relationship with adults
22. Students are always ready and hungry to learn and to absorb new information, ideas, and techniques
23. Students know that their contributions are important
24. Students know that their good performance will be rewarded through both intrinsic and extrinsic ways
    Your Comparison

Table 6.4.   A Comparison of Athletic and Academic Practices

Athletic Coaches	Academic Teachers	
		Question #19
		Question #20
		Question #21
		Question #22
		Question #23
		Question #24

25. Students know and agree with the organizational vision and goals
26. Students know that teamwork is important even when attempting to reach individual goals
27. Students are allowed and expected to assist others who may not be as talented
28. Students know that their preparation and efforts will pay off in the long run
29. Students develop great pride and self confidence each and every day of participation
30. Students believe that adults have their best interest at heart and trust them to make good decisions on their behalf.
    Your Comparison

Table 6.5.   A Comparison of Athletic and Academic Practices

Athletic Coaches	Academic Teachers	
		Question #25
		Question #26
		Question #27
		Question #28
		Question #29
		Question #30

There is growing sentiment in many progressive public schools that one should embrace many of the beliefs and practices of the more successful athletic coaches and immediately apply them to academic settings. There is no question that these themes will go a long way in developing a relationship with many school age males. There is currently no acceptable academic language that far too many of today's young men can identify with and feel comfortable embracing while attending America's public schools.

There is currently a growing communications rift between the predominantly female instructors and their male students. We need to adapt many of the organizational ideas and philosophies that have made successful coaches so beloved and respected over the years. It is not just about more money and physical power over students. It is more about connecting with young men and getting them to buy into the academic goals of our classrooms. American public schools must move boys toward the goal of becoming scholar-athletes and not allow them to separate themselves into narrowly focused niches that allows for little intellectual growth.

Coaching is considered a "helping relationship" where one person using proven methods and models of human and organizational development, engages others in discovering, accessing, and leveraging their abilities to achieve personal and organizational excellence. Coaching is a goal-oriented, solution focused process in which the coach works with others to help identify and construct possible solutions, delineate a range of goals and options, and facilitate the development and enactment of action plans to achieve those goals.

TRANSITIONING FROM
TEACHERS TO ACADEMIC COACHES

Teachers must evolve from being solely subject area teachers into becoming "Academic Coaches." There is currently far too much negative symbolism connected with being a teacher in too many of America's public schools today. We must develop a new system of educational language and endearing terms that connect with 21st century students, especially boys.

Meeting the needs of a wide range of students is hard work! There are many misperceptions about what differentiation entails. It does not always mean individualized instruction. You don't create twenty different lessons for your twenty students! The best way to imagine differentiating for various learner needs is to watch what good coaches do. They use a common sense in managing and grouping kids. Good coaches consistently do the following:

1. Good coaches narrow the instructional range (flexible grouping based on skill level).
2. Good coaches maintain high standards (they don't lower the hoop so everyone can make a basket).
3. Good coaches allow students to set their own pace and excel to the level at which they are capable (they don't ask the fastest athletes to slow down and wait for the others to catch up).
4. Good coaches have a common purpose but supporting individual strengths. Once you've learned how to play the sport, focus on your strengths for example if you're a good quarterback, you don't have to spend hours perfecting your goal kicking skills).
5. Good coaches encourage students to achieve their personal best by assessing where they are and setting goals for improvement.
6. Good coaches allow different groups to be working on different skills at the same time.
7. Good coaches encourage working together as a team and analyzing efforts in order to continually improve.

Some of these strategies are not yet widespread in the classroom, such as, grouping by skill level. There remains a reluctance to allow students of similar ability to work together. Many experts suggest that we use the athletic model as a source of inspiration in managing classrooms; our students would have a greater sense of empowerment and efficacy. This would be difficult but rewarding for both the teacher and the students. Instruction is not individualized, but it is more personalized because it is aimed at the learner's needs. It allows for more student choice and decision-making in the learning process. It may initially appear to be more work for the teacher, but it actually puts more responsibility on the student. Small group work is more inspiring because it encourages students to give their personal best which means that everybody benefits.

Academic Coaching

The role shifts from one of control of what and how students learn to one of mediation of student learning. This new coaching role requires the teacher to be as engaged in learning as their students and to develop a new sensitivity in our teaching beliefs, actions, and decisions. There are instructional principles that can guide the practice of teaching and the design of learning environments. Educators must learn to anchor all learning activities to a larger task or problem. All effective 21st century teachers must do the following:

1. Support the learning in developing ownership for the overall problem or task.
2. Design authentic tasks.
3. Design the task and the learning environment to reflect the complexity of the environment they should be able to function in at the end of learning.
4. Give the learner ownership of the process used to develop a solution.
5. Design the learning environment to support and challenge the learner's thinking.
6. Encourage testing ideas against alternative views and alternative contexts.
7. Providing opportunity for and support reflection on both the content learned and the learning process.

Making the transition from teacher as information-giver to teacher as coach is challenging and requires learning new skills. The new role as coach requires teachers to learn how to question students' thinking and to challenge students to support their conclusions.

Teaching and Coaching—Is There a Difference?

The terms teaching and coaching are often used interchangeable to imply the transference of knowledge of a subject from one person (the teacher or coach) to another (the student or athlete). The two terms are not strictly interchangeable and sometimes have different meanings. Teaching tends to be a mainly one-way process. The teacher transfers his or her knowledge to the pupil. The pupil may question in order to clarify, however the knowledge transfer is all one-way.

Coaching is a two-way process. The coach provides the athlete with the benefit of his or her knowledge and experience. The athlete then takes as much or as little of that information to use in their training. There are different levels of coaching from group coaching where the general aim is consistent to one-to-one coaching where the aim is specific to that individual.

Another difference between teaching and coaching is that with coaching there is often less focus on the acquisition of skills than in the improvement of existing skills and also fitness. It is about getting the full potential from the athlete in their chosen sport through the application of knowledge and a two-way communication process.

NEVER STOP LEARNING

There has been much debate as to whether or not the boy problem in public schools is real or perceived. Many experts conclude that the educational achievement gap is real and has serious social, economic, and political consequences. The situation is by no means hopeless! We must start looking at the problem in new ways and avoid simplistic one-shot solutions. The discussion of any social problem that is analyzed on the basis of how different ethnic groups compare is no longer considered odd. Statistics for whites are usually taken as a measure of the natural state of society, and black statistics are used as a measure of the problem. There are some who wish to resolve the problem by getting black children to act white in their behaviors, mannerisms, and values.

This is irrespective of the positive virtues that emanate from the black community. It is highly unlikely that rejecting the black behavior model will give students the satisfaction and chances of economic and educational success in life. There are dramatic differences in attitudes toward academic and career success between the generation of blacks that came of age during the civil rights struggle and their children when studying black high school students.

Many experts strongly believe that intelligence can be taught and that students can be taught to perform better academically by a suitably planned program that stresses the importance of higher-level thinking skills. Xavier University (New Orleans, LA) adopted an inspired curriculum for their incoming freshmen which resulted in improved academic performance so much that Xavier is now one of the single biggest suppliers of black graduates to medical schools, despite its relatively small enrollment. This program stressed the challenging nature of the academic program, the drive for excellence as opposed to remediation. The theme of continuous academic challenge should be a goal of every public school in America.

We can no longer allow our children to be entertained by a "Sage on a Stage." The best teaching practices of progressive educators empowers students to take control and to become more responsible for their own education.

Alternative active learning methods of education (inquiry learning) use intrinsic rewards as the primary motivator for students. They are motivated by their own efforts to solve complex and challenging problems. Most humans experience a deep feeling a pleasure and joy after successfully tackling a complex problem. There is extreme pride in one's personal accomplishments. Unfortunately, this happens far too rarely in public schools across America. Instead, many students (irrespective of gender or ethnicity) see the classroom as a place where they are made to learn material and jump through assessment hoops that have no meaning for them, with the carrot being rewarding employment far into the future.

It is our growing responsibility to assist our students to embrace and to understand this important transition in their young life. Research indicates that active learning methods produce significant academic gains for students with more on-task behavior in class. These methods also reduce the achievement gap. It reduces the urge to dumb down the curriculum or to depress the performance of traditional high achievers. The most dramatic gains tend to be for those who are not well served by the traditional passive model. This is because these students are the ones who lagged behind more in the traditional classroom and thus have more room to improve their performance.

Modern research concludes that there have consistently been a relatively small percentage of students (20–30%) from families that expect them to attend college. The extrinsic motivator for these students and families is the link between effort, credentials, and rewards. Students understood that they must maintain discipline, attend classes, and graduate even when colleges and subjects are not challenging or intellectually stimulating. Students avoided the wrath of parents and family and entered the adult world having at least accomplished something in their short life span. They eventually learned to adjust and to develop higher order thinking skills once they secured a job. The link between effort and reward is weaker and extrinsic rewards are far less robust for many children in America. For the low socio income students and families of color, these extrinsic motivators for academic effort and excellence are often less compelling.

There are some researchers who theorize that the effort/reward link may at times work against education because life on the street may appear to be more realistic and offer more tangible benefits when comparing the two. The American public school system is relegated to producing a large number of uneducated people as long as little value is placed on expecting all students to reach their full intellectual potential. The academic achievement gap in America will continue to grow in communities of color until a fundamental change in the delivery of educational services is implemented across the board.

There is no doubt that the decline of America's public schools is real and becoming a growing challenge. We must begin to acknowledge that structural changes that must immediately take place if our children are to reach their true potential and become viable, productive, global citizen and leaders. There is no greater way to highlight this sense of urgency in closing the achievement gap than to carefully examine the following story of the canary in the coal mine.

Years ago coal miners took canaries into the mines as detectors of noxious gases. If the canary died, then the miners realized that they were in a region of danger and took the necessary precautions. The academic performance of the black/brown community is like the canary, and the coal mine is the educational system. The warning signals are apparent. Treating the problem by trying to make blacks "like whites" would be like replacing the canary in the coal mine with a bird that is more resistant to poisonous gases. It simply ignores the real problem.

America must acknowledge the grave state of affairs surrounding the challenge of closing the achievement gap. Frivolous, shallow analyses will do more harm than good. It forces well intentioned professionals to choose between two unpalatable options. They can look for shortcomings in the character or culture of the involuntary minority community or they can adopt race-neutral socioeconomic explanations. Neither choice is comprehensive enough to address the challenges within American public schools. Closing the achievement gap is growing concern. It is complex and historically rooted in ethnic relationships and communities. We must not view this problem as being impossible to resolve. We must begin to look at these problems with a new cultural lens of old and new strategies. We must not be drawn to feel good, simplistic, one shot solutions.

"You get from people what you expect."

—Author Unknown

VERBAL AND NONVERBAL CUES

There is a growing belief that teachers and male students seem to oftentimes be speaking a different language to each other. There is also a belief that many current teachers who were trained and educated under the increasingly outdated 20th century model have refused to make the necessary adjustments to reconnect with 21st century students. There is extensive discussion about the essential need to retrain teachers to become more proficient in recognizing and interpreting verbal and non verbal cues by their male students. Much valuable information is transmitted without words. Skillful use of nonverbal behaviors is essential in communicating attitudes necessary for establishing and maintaining positive relationships such as interest, acceptance, warmth are powerful as a tool in clarifying, emphasizing the meaning of verbal messages.

Many professionals are aware that body language and voice reflections can influence communication, but the impact of nonverbal behaviors is greater than you may have suspected. Words used in your communication may convey far less information than do the nonverbal components. The full impact of an individual's spoken message may be broken down as follows:

1. 7% verbal components
2. 38% vocal (volume, pitch, rhythm) components and
3. 55% facial expression

People communicate nonverbally in several ways. Three primary classes of nonverbal cues are:

1. Body movements, such as facial expression, eye contact, posture, and gestures:
2. Vocal cues, such as quality of voice and the pacing or flow of speech: and
3. Spatial relations, which include the physical distance between the participants. Minimal encouragers form a fourth class of nonverbal cues, even though they contain verbal components. Each of these categories of cues affects the nature of the communication between people

It is both confusing and frustrating when teachers cannot effectively communicate with the very students they are being paid to educate. This scenario is being played out in public schools all across America each day. The growing diversity that is so pronounced in our country is here to stay! Effective non verbal skills are just as important to the success of many students and teachers as verbal communication. There seems to be a growing disconnect in how traditional middle class teachers interpret their students non verbal expressions and what is really intended by 21st century male students.

It does not take much imagination to visualize the growing disjointed classroom settings taking place throughout this nation because of a spiraling misinterpretation of non verbal cues by both adults and students. Boys all across America are being victimized by well intentioned adults because of this misunderstanding. Much has been written about the language challenges of immigrants but, not enough solutions have been shared about the non language behaviors that are having a dramatically negative impact on learning in 21st century American classrooms.

In recent years we have seen an avalanche of studies regarding the declining academic achievement of boys. We are just now grasping the full magnitude of these concerns. We acknowledge their gradual intellectual decline but little ideas have been put forward as systematic solutions for consideration. There is little doubt that boys have changed dramatically over the past 20–30 years. The typical belief is that boys have undergone a tumultuous change if for no other reason than the dramatic increase in the number of single female run parent households and the soaring divorce rate. There are a variety of other causes chief among which is the growing rate of poverty students in American public schools.

All of these themes have underscored the dearth of positive male role models that exist in the lives of boys today. The informal cues of being taught the proper way to respond to a given situation are not being handed down like in previous generations (Oral Traditions). In the past, educators could always assume that boys had been taught the basics of how to play the game called school. There was an unspoken code of acceptable behavior that just about everyone knew and adhered to. That stream of knowledge has been irretrievably interrupted and can never be assumed to exist anymore. Adults must rethink their assumptions regarding 21st century boys and put systems into place that begin to make sense in addressing this growing national dilemma.

The No Child Left Behind (NCLB) law has placed demands on all educators regarding the goal of meeting the academic needs of all students, even our boys. We can no longer take for granted that adults totally understand a boy's needs, learning styles, and desires. The learning environment has changed and unfortunately, many of America's public schools have failed to remain current. It is the responsibility of all professional educators to reach out to build the kinds of relationships that make sense to males.

Boys have internalized a new value system that is very foreign to many of our traditional teachers in American public education classrooms. Stephen Covey's, "7 Habits of Highly Effective People" notes that it is the responsibility of professional educators to seek first to understand and then to be understood. Therein lies the real problems. We no longer truly understand the very boys who appear in our classrooms everyday.

This author developed a nationwide survey (www.edtransform.com) to gather cultural differences and attitudinal data about today's males. We have far too long resisted the seas of change that has taken place in males across this country. We assume too much about the value system of our young men and are disappointed in them when they do not measure up to the beliefs of the past. Many boys, however, have been taught anti social behaviors that conflict with the traditional ways of conducting school business in the past. Those were the schools where children were seen and rarely heard.

All educators must become better people watchers if we are to better understand today's children. We must learn to rely more on our interpretation of their body gestures and other unspoken words to provide us with relevant clues regarding the mindset of boys. Professionals responsible for the intellectual well being of our young men must stay verbally and nonverbally connected during these difficult times.

Nonverbal Communication Modes

Nonverbal communication involves those nonverbal stimuli in a communication setting. It is sending and receiving messages in a variety of ways without the use of verbal codes (words). It is both intentional and unintentional. Most speakers and listeners are not conscious of this. It includes many of the following terms:

- glance
- eye contact (gaze)
- touch
- volume
- vocal nuance
- proximity
- gestures
- facial expression pause (silence)
- intonation
- dress
- posture
- smell
- word choice and syntax
- sounds (paralanguage)
- chest bump
- knuckle bump

Non verbal interaction is important because it is one of the key aspects of communication (and especially important in a high-context culture). It has multiple functions:

- Repeat the verbal message by pointing in a direction while stating directions.
- Often complement the verbal message but also may contradict. A nod reinforces a positive message (among Americans); a "wink" may contradict a stated positive message.
- Regulate interactions (non-verbal cues convey when the other person should speak or not speak).
- May substitute for the verbal message especially if it is blocked by noise or interruption, gestures by finger to lips to indicate need for quiet), facial expressions such as a nod instead of a yes.

Note the implications of the proverb: "Actions speak louder than words." This underscores the importance of non-verbal communication. Non-verbal communication is especially significant in intercultural situations. Non-verbal differences account for typical difficulties in communicating.

Male Nonverbal Cues

- A half nod—bye
- Half smile—Hi
- Shake hands—good job
- Wink—good luck
- Nodding head up—hello
- Rolling eyes—annoyed or I can't believe that
- Staring at someone—they need to be quiet
- Shrugging shoulders—I don't know
- Nod—What's up?
- Shaking head—can't believe it
- Gesturing to yourself—come over here
- "Evil" eye—mad
- "Ahem"—listen
- Thumbs up—good
- Thumbs down—bad
- Two hands covering your neck—whatever is happening is "choking" you
- Pounding your fist—angry
- Pounding someone else's fist—good job
- Moving open hand back and forth—Maybe

- Looking away—not going to look you in the eye
- Sucking with your teeth—don't really agree with you
- Look at the ceiling or floor—don't really know answer
- Start rocking—sensory overload
- Hit, touch, each other
- Blowing up at you—make yourself bigger than you actually are. Like a Puffer Fish
- Bowing of head—that's ok
- Whistling—happy
- Palm Up—don't understand
- Fist Bumping—Solidarity

BOYS AND GIRLS LEARN DIFFERENTLY

Much has been written about the difference between boys and girls in recent years. There has been extensive "Brain Based" research that outlines radical learning and behavioral style differences between boys and girls. Boys are generally more aggressive and respond louder than girls. This typically is not the preferred learning style of America's public schools predominantly female teaching staff. There has been much new information generated about the differences between the male and female brain functions. Boys tend to be deductive in their conceptualizations, starting their reasoning process frequently from a general principle and applying it, or ancillary principles, to individual cases.

They also tend to do deductive reasoning more quickly than girls. This is a reason that boys, on average, do better on fast, rapid fire multiple-choice tests, for instance on the Scholastic Aptitude Tests. The better a person is at making a quick deduction; the better he or she does on the test that relies on this skill.

Boys tend to be better than girls at not seeing or touching the thing and yet still being able to calculate it. For example, when mathematics is taught on the chalkboard boys often do better at it than girls. When it is taught using manipulative and objects taken off the board, out of the abstract world of signs and signifiers, and put into the concrete world of physical number chains. The female brain often finds it easier.

Males like abstract philosophical arguments, philosophical, conundrums, and moral debates about abstract principles. There are many exceptions to all these rules. Females do produce more words than males at an earlier age. During the learning process, girls often use words as they learn, and boys often work silently. Even when we study student group processes, we find females in a learning group using words more often than males. We also find that word users in the male group tend to be fewer. Generally one or two dominant males use a lot of words, and the other males far fewer, whereas there is more parity in word use among the female group. Whether its language from sports trivia, the law, or the military, boys tend to work out codes among themselves and within their own cognation process, and rely on coded language to communicate.

Boys get bored more easily than girls and often require more and varying stimulants to keep them attentive. Girls are better at self-managing boredom during instruction and all aspects of education. This has a profound impact on all aspects of learning. Once the child has become bored, he is likely not only to give up on learning but also to act out in such a way that class is disrupted and he is labeled a behavioral problem. Girls do not generally need to move around as much while learning. Movement seems to help boys not only stimulate their brains but also manage and relieve impulsive behavior. Movement is also natural to boys in a closed space, thanks to their higher metabolism, which created fidgeting behavior.

Many teachers find that the one or two boys who can't stop moving in class can be managed by putting them to work, such as letting them hand out papers or go sharpen pencils for the teacher. Stretch breaks and sixty-second movement breaks are very helpful to all students at any age. Teachers often find that allowing a boy to play with something (silently) in his hand, such as a nerf ball, while he's learning can help. He's moving, his brain is being stimulated, he feels comfortable and not distracting any body else.

The following chart highlights some generalized differences between the Genders

Table 6.6. Differences between the Genders

Males	Females
Extrinsic Learners	Intrinsic Learners
Impulsive	Self Motivated
Fidgety	Short Term Memory
Abstract Reasoning	Inductive Thinking
Spatial Relationships	Better Writers
Deductive Reasoning	Better Listeners
Better in Math	Better in Reading
Movement works best	Note Taking Skills
Thrives on Academic Competition	Enjoys some Academic Competition

There is a much more sinister question being discussed in both private and public educational circles. Should our public schools operate more efficiently or more effectively? To be more efficient does not mean that schools are more effective. On the contrary, data indicates that in reference to males, public schools are not nearly effective enough! The answer in many circles is that far too many schools are still committed to 20th century methodologies. We are not meeting the educational needs of untold millions of 21st century students each and every day.

That is why we continue to have a growing dropout problem (2 million plus each year since 2005). Schools now have serious competition with charter schools, home schooling, and private, parochial, and on-line technology schools. Public schools no longer have a monopoly and must make the necessary adjustments to recapture the hearts and minds of our children, parents and taxpayers.

America is falling further and further behind our industrialized and international competition regarding the quality of education that emanates from many public schools. The efficiency of our school transportation, food service, building maintenance, business services and personnel management departments means very little if American children continue to graduate unable to function in the increasingly high tech and highly competitive world Global Society. The United States public school academic performance must be dramatically ratcheted upward if we are to maintain our nation's high standard of living.

We must reward educators who are willing to take well thought out and well planned academic risks in order to prepare our increasingly at risk students for real world 21st century global challenges. This does not require unlimited sums of money to accomplish this educational mission. It does necessitate that we embrace new ideas and concepts that make organizational sense. We must think more "Out of the Box." The growth of gender based education classes is one such change. This idea has been in existence for hundreds of years but, was only recently permitted again by the United States Department of Education in 2006. Gender based classrooms were banned in the USA during the early 1970s as a response to the expanding 'Women's Movement.'

The Title IX law was enacted as a way to catch the girls up to the built in advantages that males had experienced for hundreds of years. This made sense at that time and girls made outstanding gains on all fronts. About the same time that this much needed attention was being given to girls the boys were entering a dramatic reduction in overall academic performance. This decline has accelerated in recent years to where it has now reached Tsunami like proportions. We can no longer ignore the statistics regarding boys. We must act and systematically address this very complex issue.

Title IX was the first major, comprehensive federal law that prohibited discrimination on the basis of sex against students and employees of educational institutions. It stated that both men and women must receive fair and equal treatment in all areas of operation within educational programs. This essentially began to level the playing field between boys and girls all across America. It began as a measure to apply equal sums of money to athletics at the college level and evolved into something much more comprehensive.

The problem today is that too many young men all across America have dramatically reduced their involvement in anything related to academics while attending public schools. Boys have carved out a narrow niche that is both limiting and fatalistic. They perform well on the fields and courts of athletic competition but, have been unable to transition these talents into the academic classrooms. It is incumbent for concerned, caring adults to assist these young men in making this sometimes frightening leap of faith. Many enlightened school leaders and teachers have adopted the belief that maintaining the "Status Quo" is no longer a viable option. We must move forward with all deliberate speed and dispatch. One of the most sobering realizations is that all current school personnel must be retrained. This presents new opportunities in our school improvement efforts that should be embraced widespread all across America.

There are more advantages than disadvantages when implementing gender education classes. The biggest advantage to all boy classrooms is that they can focus on the academic lessons and resist flirting with girls. The second biggest advantage is that their intellectual energy is now concentrated by way of academic competition. The one big disadvantage is that there is sometimes an overload of testosterone in a classroom which necessitates a demand and expectation of well trained teachers. These professionals must understand and adhere to specific learning styles and teaching strategies that work best for boys.

DEFINING GENDER EDUCATION

Gender education is the behavioral, cultural, or psychological traits typically associated with one sex. Campbell Middle School (Cobb County Georgia) was the first public school in Metro Atlanta to incorporate the separation of boys and girls classes with a great deal of academic success in 2002–2003. This large, underperforming, diverse school had the following demographics:

1. 1400 Students
2. 50% African Americans students
3. 37% Latino students
4. 13% Caucasian students

5. 44% Transient students
6. 86% Free and reduced lunch
7. 70% Single parent households
8. 35% of Boys had juvenile records or probation officers
9. 85% of Discipline problems were caused by boys
10. 90% of Special education students were boys
11. 30% of the lowest CRCT scores were by boys
12. 25% of male students failed to be promoted without failing grades

WHY GENDER EDUCATION WORKS!

One of the great joys of many of the most effective gender based teachers is that they enjoy great instructional freedom. As long as they follow the core curriculum, teachers are granted latitude while using proven gender education strategies. There are no scripted lesson plans. You must bring your 'A Game" each day when engaging a classroom of boys.

The theme "Why Boys are Falling Behind Girls in Education" was examined from a business perspective and what it meant for the economy, business and society. It stated that boys typically develop fine motor skills up to six years later than girls and those boys tend to be unfairly compared with girls during the early years. It noted that schools should be playing to boy's strength, such as playing games, building forts out of blocks, kicking a soccer ball, rather than emphasizing their weaknesses. It concluded that if the creeping pattern of male disengagement and economic dependency continues, more men could end up becoming losers in a global economy that values mental power over might.

Before educators, corporations, and policymakers can narrow the new gender gap, they have to understand its myriad causes. Experts noted everything from absentee parenting to the lack of male teachers to corporate takeovers of lunch rooms. Some believe boys are responding to cultural signals such as downsized dads casts adrift in the 'New Economy,' a dumb and dumber dude culture that demeans academic achievement, and the glamorization of all things gangster that makes school seem so un cool.

Many experts conclude that schools have inadvertently played a big role too, losing sight of boys by taking for granted that they were doing well, even though the data began to show the opposite. Many administrators saw boys, rather than the way schools were treating them, as the problem. Instead of catering to boys' learning styles many schools are force fitting them into an unnatural mold. The current sit-still-and listen paradigm isn't ideal for either sex. Instead of recommending medication, experts say educators should focus on helping boys feel less like undesirables. The gender gap also has roots in the expectation gap. In the 1970s, boys were far more likely to anticipate getting a college degree and girls satisfied in the cheerleader role. Today, girls' expectations are spiraling, while boys are plummeting at an alarming rate.

HOW AMERICAN PUBLIC SCHOOLS ARE HARMING BOYS

There is a growing band of researchers that believe that public schools are actually hurting boys? The following facts have been noted regarding public schools.

1. By third grade too many boys are already falling behind in the classroom
2. Around third and fourth grade, there is a shift in the way teachers instruct kids.
3. This change in the teaching approach, from an informal, learning by doing style to the more structured, sit down and listen up, is toughest on male students, who tend to be more active in elementary and middle schools.
4. There is often an undercurrent of fear or tension between male students and female teachers.
5. On some subliminal level, the teacher is afraid to have even a very young male defy the simplest rule. He or she is afraid his defiance will escalate.
6. By fourth grade this boy may have already given up on school especially if he hasn't yet learned to read.
7. As a general rule, children, especially boys tend to live up or down to adult expectations, and it doesn't take very long for students to detect how much or how little is expected of them.
8. Parents believe that stereotypes creep into many teachers' perceptions.
9. Many teachers hold fast to certain assumptions about how male students are supposed to behave. If it does not fit into their model, they oftentimes put that kid down.

All of these beliefs results in the emergence of hostile attitudes on the part of both boys and the public school teaching staff.

Why Do Boys Come To Public Schools Today?

Years ago boys would come to school for the following reasons:

1. To become educated and prepare for the future.
2. To participate in sports.
3. To interact with adults and peers (socialization).

Recent research suggests that 21st century boys come to school for the following reasons:

1. To flirt with girls.
2. To play sports.
3. To eat (breakfast, lunch, after school snacks).
4. To socialize, fight, gang bang.
5. To become educated and prepare for the future.

This author wrote "Gender Education in 7 Steps: Reigniting the Academic Pilot Lights of Boys and Girls" published in 2007. It chronicled the introduction of the sometimes misunderstood school improvement effort. It listed the steps that are necessary for a new concept to be successfully implemented in any public school setting. Schools must evaluate where they currently stand academically and then decide what strategies to implement. This author suggests that you examine the following set of indices:

1. The number and percentage of boys who are at the bottom 25% of most major standardized test scores (CRCT, SAT, ITBS, High School Graduation rates, etc)
2. The number and percentage of boys who have discipline problems in school.
3. The number and percentage of males teaching academic subjects.
4. The number and percentage of students with two parent families.
5. The overall attitude of the faculty (high or low expectations).
6. The number and percentage of students already involved with the Juvenile Justice system.
7. The number and percentage of teacher and student turnover.
8. The type of leadership within the building (take charge, laissez faire, etc)
9. The up to date review of staff development programs for effectiveness
10. The number and percentage of boys in special education classes.

Boys, even more than girls are in serious trouble today once you examine data over the past 20 years. There is now a serious crisis among males, the likes we have never seen before. A growing number of males are struggling with perplexing social pressures and forces that yesterday's children didn't have to face. Gender based education research strategies work because they isolate the problems and play to the strengths of both boys and girls. The following teaching strategies have had widespread success when applied to gender based boys classrooms. It is my belief that system wide retraining of all teachers is needed if we are to successfully tackle this problem. "Gender

How to motivate and teach the challenging, diverse, at-risk student is a universal academic problem that demands to be addressed as we move further into the 21st Century. Why can't these students meet high academic and performance standards? Is it because education has failed to stay current with new research-based ideas and to embrace trends that are gaining support? Or is it the day-to-day minutiae that engulfs many of our at-risk teachers and robs them of their energy and self-confidence to take educational risks and try new and innovative proposals?

Gender Education in 7 Steps

is designed for those practioners, parents and citizens who have a genuine interest and concern about the state of public schools across America. Our emphasis on cutting-edge 21st Century ideas is only surpassed by embracing and adopting concepts from our past, such as gender education. Only by combining the best of both worlds (past and present educational concepts) can we begin to put public education back on a path toward excellence!

This book adds extremely relevant knowledge and skills for innovative reformers and more traditional leaders alike. It provides a solid set of interesting methodologies and 21st Century strategies and suggestions that can be used immediately by practicing school administrators.
—Dr. J. Eric Tubbs, Asst. Professor, Kennesaw State University

This is a must-read book for educators that will innovate and motivate. It addresses the issues that face gender-based learning, and provides an insight to how and why it works.
—Michael Tappler, PhD
Principal, Marietta's 1st Charter School

$19.95

Gender Education in 7 Steps:

Reigniting the Academic Pilot Lights of Boys and Girls

H. E. Holliday, PhD

Education in 7 Steps" outlines the process by which to implement this radical form of restructuring.

Teaching Strategies That Work for Boys

- Jigsaw Puzzles, Crossword Puzzles (must use your imagination)
- Beat the Clock Game Format (time element)
- Friendly competition by groups/teams
- Family groupings of four
- Positive reinforcement
- Varied activities geared toward the male interest
- Manipulative/Hands on activities
- Graphic Organizers
- Assignments involving technology
- Promote Quick starting lessons on time
- Athletic themes for academic activities
- Rubrics
- Playing Chess (must strategize before acting)

Teaching Strategies to Avoid for Boys

- Large Classes
- Long Projects
- KISS (keep it short and simple)
- Long note taking assignments
- Prolonged Group Work Assignments
- Negative Criticism
- Long Periods of Quiet Work
- Prolonged Teacher Lecturing
- Down Time before or during class
- Lack of Structure in classes
- Lack of Teaching From Bell to Bell
- Worksheets

There is a growing body of evidence that suggest that there is a toxic relationship between far too many boys and far too many teachers when examining public schools today. Boys are being psychologically harmed by the following actions of adults:

1. Cultural insensitivity
2. Lowered Expectations
3. Unduly harsh discipline
4. The systemic shunting of boys into remedial or special education classes.

The term Micro Inequities occurs when small slights lead to huge problems in the diverse workplace. These behaviors have been internalized by both male students and their female teachers. These nearly invisible signals can have a dramatic impact on work relationships. The greatest power of micro inequity messages may be their influence on building up, or breaking down, relationships between teens and parents, between husbands and wives, between students and teachers, between administrators and faculty and among friends.

American public schools face numerous challenges when addressing the boy challenge. The three most immediate goals are as follows:

1. To greatly reduce the soaring drop out rates of all students, but especially boys.
2. To better control, service, and reduce the growing cost of educating special education students (90% are boys).
3. To implement effective teaching strategies that emphasizes best practices for male students at all grade levels.

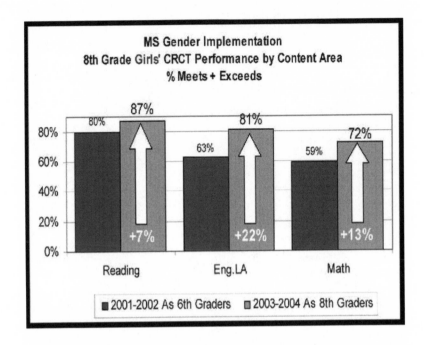

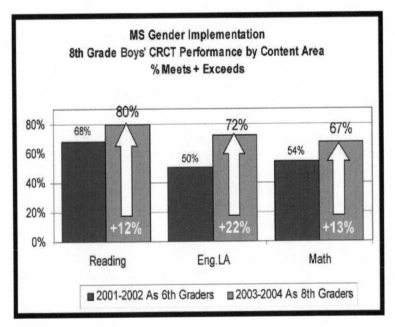

Graph 6.1. MS Gender Implementation

One of the greatest local school based cost centers revolves around the special education programs. The following facts are readily determined when reviewing the special education challenges:

1. Special Education consumes a significant percentage of many public school budgets.
2. There seems to be no definitive way of reducing that number or ensuring the academic success of special education Students.
3. Too many traditional instructors are reluctant to embrace the Inclusion/Co Teaching Model because of a dearth of research.
4. 90% of special education students are boys.
5. Many of these students have decidedly reduced academic expectations imposed on them by their teachers.
6. Once put into these special education classes students rarely reach their true academic potential.

The following Student Achievement Pyramid (Response to Intervention) is a good visualization of how we must begin to address the whole child. This illustration presents a snapshot of the successful stages when initiating systematic special education strategies in public schools.

Recent research strongly suggests that gender education classes work best when addressing special education challenges for the following reasons:

1. The Mainstreaming or Co Teaching Model puts two well trained instructors in the same class where many of the best practice strategies work best.
2. *Tier 1* of the Pyramid emphasizes (Differentiated Instruction) and Standards Based classroom instruction and 183 learning. Gender education excels at promoting specific strategies designed for boys in that classroom.
3. *Tier II* of the Pyramid emphasizes (small group work or cooperative learning), and needs based instruction/learning Intervention protocol. Gender education is best implemented when classes are broken into small learning groups that encourages greater interaction and builds community among students.
4. *Tier III* of the Pyramid is tailored to meet the specific learning needs of the boys in that gender based class.

Special Education Students can now be fully incorporated into Gender specific classes thereby further reducing the need for pull out classes and teachers. This results in a tremendous educational savings for schools and districts.

By incorporating special education students into gender based classes we now have high expectations for all students without reservations. A good

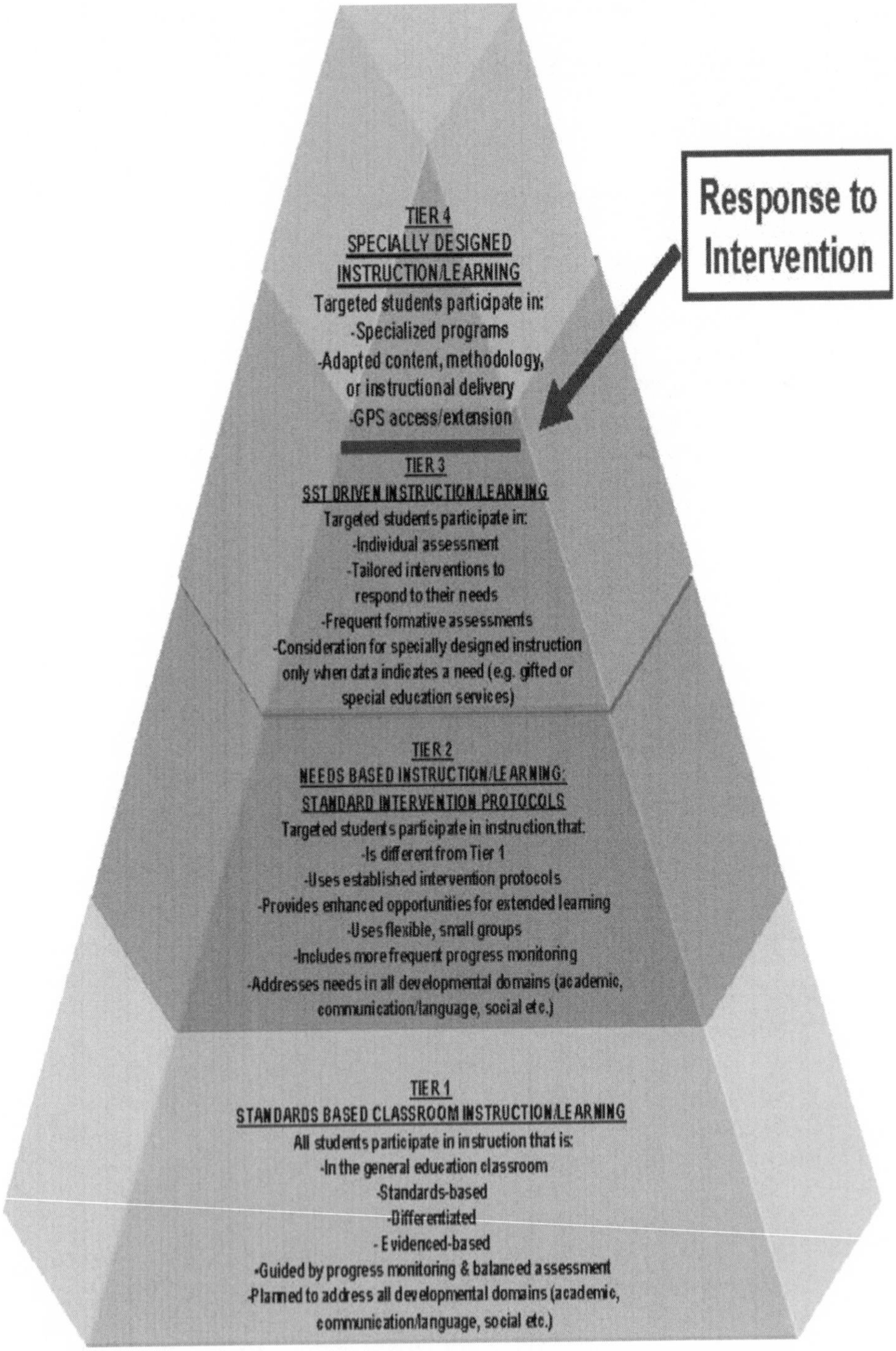

Response to Intervention

TIER 4
SPECIALLY DESIGNED
INSTRUCTION/LEARNING
Targeted students participate in:
-Specialized programs
-Adapted content, methodology,
or instructional delivery
-GPS access/extension

TIER 3
SST DRIVEN INSTRUCTION/LEARNING
Targeted students participate in:
-Individual assessment
-Tailored interventions to
respond to their needs
-Frequent formative assessments
-Consideration for specially designed instruction
only when data indicates a need (e.g. gifted or
special education services)

TIER 2
NEEDS BASED INSTRUCTION/LEARNING:
STANDARD INTERVENTION PROTOCOLS
Targeted students participate in instruction that:
-Is different from Tier 1
-Uses established intervention protocols
-Provides enhanced opportunities for extended learning
-Uses flexible, small groups
-Includes more frequent progress monitoring
-Addresses needs in all developmental domains (academic,
communication/language, social etc.)

TIER 1
STANDARDS BASED CLASSROOM INSTRUCTION/LEARNING
All students participate in instruction that is:
-In the general education classroom
-Standards-based
-Differentiated
- Evidenced-based
-Guided by progress monitoring & balanced assessment
-Planned to address all developmental domains (academic,
communication/language, social etc.)

Graph 6.2. Student Achievement Pyramid of Interventions

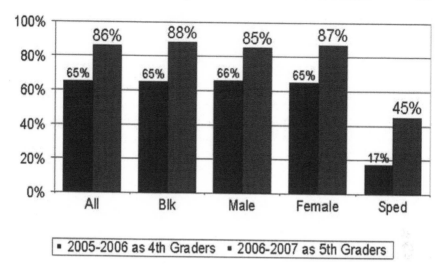

Graph 6.3.

frame of reference is to examine what happens to special education students on school athletic teams. All football, basketball, baseball, and soccer team members are expected to learn the same plays, as well as the rules if they want to play more. We must develop the same high academic expectations if we are to truly raise the educational bar for America's Public Schools. When

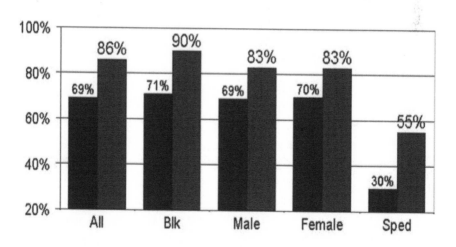

Graph 6.4.

examining the special education (Sped) statistics in the following gender based classes you can readily see dramatic improvement using the teaching strategies that make sense to boys. The academic growth of the Sped students was exponential.

> "The art of teaching is the art of assisting discovery. You can teach a lesson for a day but if you teach curiosity, you teach for a lifetime. It's too bad that the people who really know how to run the country are busy teaching school. When truth stands in the way, you are headed in the wrong direction. When teaching the love of truth, never lose the truth of love."
>
> —Unknown Author

21ST CENTURY STUDENT DISCIPLINE

One of the greatest challenges for adults in the field of education is how to manage student behavior. There can be no consistent high quality learning without a school wide discipline program in place. There are a variety of commercial disciplined based programs available for purchase. One rule of thumb when addressing any student is to preserve their dignity and respect at all times. Treating all students consistently is essential in this multicultural world today. Adults must be role models at all times by never practicing bad behavior or accepting it from students or other adults. We must become more proactive in addressing this all encompassing dilemma that helps to define the culture of a school. There can be little productivity in school without hard fast rules, regulations, and procedures followed by all participants. Parents want only a few deliverables from most schools. They are as follows:

1. A safe orderly environment
2. A strong academic program
3. A chance to become involved as a true and valued partner

Why do so many students continue to act out is a relevant question that needs further examination? The following are the most consistent answers:

1. Attention (many students see classrooms as an opportunity to gain easy attention after being ignored and considered to be disposable early in their young lives).
2. Power (many students see classrooms as a means to acquire and assume power over ineffective adults. This is survival of the fittest where only the strong survive in the mindset of a child).

3. Revenge (many students see this as a time to seek revenge or vindication for past adult injustices. They seek to inflict pain and suffering on others to atone for their own long suffering circumstances.
4. Fear of Failure: many students will not allow themselves to suffer further humiliation by being seen as not knowing. They choose to not try rather than to care about succeeding and still failing.

The following ideas need to be pursued when designing and developing a healthy classroom learning environment. Each student should be made to feel like they belong and involved when establishing the following rules and expectations:

1. There must be freedom of limits
2. Shared responsibility
3. Structured choices
4. Self discipline is encouraged
5. Mutual respect
6. Teacher as student
7. Results equals cooperation and responsibility

It is recommended that you over prepare and only bring your 'A Game' when interacting with 21st Century students. One should be ready by consistently practicing the following:

1. Know how to respond when hearing about shocking personal experiences. Do not let on that you do not understand.
2. Always be cool, calm, collected, capable, confident, caring and consistent at all times.
3. Do not cuss, cry or complain.
4. Use humor whenever possible. Humor is often overlooked as a teaching tool and is too often overlooked in college classrooms. Laughter often releases stress and tension for both the instructor and the student. You should encourage the ability to laugh at yourself and to not take yourself so seriously. This helps to build a friendly classroom environment that facilitates learning.
5. You must maintain your youthful spirit regardless of your chronological age.

Chapter 7

Importance of Understanding

The popular recording group Sly and the Family Stone sang "You Can Make It If You Try" in 1969. The lyrics were written as a source of encouragement for individuals who may have had self doubts about their ability to flourish during that turbulent decade. It provided a catchy inspirational song that implored individuals to try hard and to never give up. This song speaks to the "Yes We Can" Attitude that propelled President Barack Obama to the 2008 Presidency. This song also speaks of personal determination and the importance of never surrendering when the going gets tough. This song served as an inspiration to even the most downtrodden, hopeless and destitute individuals. The lyrics talked passionately about the importance of attitude.

The longer one lives, the more one realizes the impact of your attitude on your life. Attitude is more important than education, than money, than circumstances, than ethnicity, success or failure. Attitude is more important than what other people think, say or do to you. It is more important than appearance, luck, or talent. Attitude will make or break a friendship, a company, a church, a home, or a school. One of the most important things humans have is a choice everyday regarding the attitude we embrace for that day. We cannot change our past and we cannot change the fact that people act in a certain way. We cannot change the inevitable. The only thing we can do is control our attitude. Experts are convinced that life is 10% what happens to you and 90% how you respond to it. We are in charge of our attitudes!

It is amazing that the United States of America with its vast amount of resources has watched the dismantling of its once vaunted public education system. It is as though we have all been asleep at the switch. Did it happen all of a sudden? Who is responsible for the current demise? What solutions seem most promising? There are many grave national concerns that are plaguing our nation and many of them are centered on our attitudes toward life. The Paradox of Our Age was written by Dr. Bob Moorehead. The poem highlighted the many numerous events that take place in our lives each day. We buy more and yet place little sentimental value on material things.

We have more medicines to take that have not made us healthier. We have more creature comforts but very little time to enjoy them. We are focused on making a dollar instead of making a difference in the lives of our children and our community. We are exposed to more and more new knowledge yet use little judgment when attempting to resolve the typical problems of the world. We profess to value our solitude and yet cannot find peace within our own families. We have high ideals and yet loose morals. All of these notions help create an atmosphere of uncertainty devoid of significant meaning within our schools and communities.

> Of True Character
> By Charles Michael Choice
> One must be totally honest in every way!
> Not only to others, but especially to yourself!
> The maze of directions we choose to follow
> as we relate to our fellow man can be difficult at best!
> It is both honesty and integrity that will
> separate us from those who distort the truth
> When others around us can be assured we are fair
> and honest, then they will put their
> total trust in you and they will not waiver
> Then and only then are we determined to be above reproach!
> We are always judged by others on how
> consistent our values are on a repetitive basis
> The path to being held in the highest
> ethical class is both short and narrow
> It does not mean you must be perfect, but
> always be honest and fair!

LESSONS CAN BE LEARNED ANYWHERE

It is amazing that lessons in life can be learned just about anywhere you go? This author was on an airplane trip to Chicago in July 1999, when my son Joshua became quite enamored with one of the many free disposable magazines available for passengers. Upon closer review, I noticed some very poignant advice when discussing the following ideas on success, imagination, leadership, excellence, and change.

The Essence of Success: If we can imagine a future then we can dream it and create it. Successful is the person who has lived well, laughed often and loved much. Successful is the person who has gained the respect of children, who leaves the world better than they found. Successful is the person who has never lacked appreciation for the earth's beauty, who never fails to look for the best in others or always give their very best.

The Essence of Imagination: You must believe it before you can conceive it. What we can see is only a small percentage of what is possible. Imagination is having the vision to see what is just below the surface: to picture that which is essential, but invisible to the eye.

The Essence of Leadership: A true leader has the confidence to stand alone, the courage to make tough decisions, and the compassion to listen to the needs of others. He does not set out to be a leader, but becomes one by the quality of his actions and the integrity of his intent. In the end, leaders are much like eagles. They don't hang in flocks because you find them one at a time.

Foundation of Excellence: When you perform above and beyond the standard. Tentative efforts lead to tentative outcomes. Commit 100% to your actions. Decide to construct your character through excellent actions and determine to pay the price of a worthy goal. The trials you encounter will introduce you to your strengths. Remain steadfast and believe that one day you will build something that is worthy of your potential.

Change: We must know why we are changing and be able to articulate where you are going as a result of this change process. If you're not riding the wave of change, you'll find yourself swept beneath it.

THE GREATEST DISCOVERY

Many experts have noted that the most important things on earth were good ideas that advanced mankind and that each of us has the capacity to initiate marvelous changes in our lives. The greatest self discovery we can make is to unlock the vast potential that lays dormant in each human being. We are what we think we are! We will become what is expected of us. We will generally rise to the expectations that are set for us. Problems develop when we set personal goals that do not offer sufficient challenges or goals that are achieved simply because the bar has been set too low.

A good example would be the sudden loss of a job that should spur much introspection and ultimately a more robust preparation for new opportunities. Far too many unemployed workers are typically conditioned to settle for just about any position once they lose their initial jobs. These individuals must prepare themselves for 21st century positions by making themselves more marketable with the acquisition of additional training. This is why we must advocate and expect to be 'Life Long Learners' for the rest of our lives.

The possible jobs available within the next ten years are not even on the drawing board at this time. We must develop a set of skills that will allow us to become active players in this increasingly high tech global society. We must learn to break the mold that defines us and to seek excellence in everything that we do. Any unemployed workers should take this opportunity to look at many exciting new options and not just yearn for the good old days. 21st century humans no longer have the luxury of sitting idly by and waiting for change to take place. The successful individual must become more proactive and make change happen!

Any person who is confronted with important decisions that will impact their future should avoid quick fix answers and look within oneself for solutions. They must raise the bar and ask the following question. What does it take to realize your true potential? Your answers should be written in detailed and with great specificity. Great leaders must display extraordinary courage. It takes courage to go against the norm and to stand in the face of challenging storms and not yield to popular demands. Courageous leaders speak their mind and have a strong moral compass.

I am reminded of a visit to Cornel University where I came upon the publicly mounted slogan of the Million Dollar Roundtable organization. These words should typify the attitude of 21st century young men throughout America.

"It is not my right to be common. If I can seek opportunity not security. I want to take the calculated risk; to dream and to build; to fail and to succeed. I refuse to barter incentive for a dole. I prefer the challenges of life to the guaranteed existence; the thrill of fulfillment to the stale calm of utopia. I will not trade freedom for benefice or my dignity for handout. I will never cower before any master nor bend to any threat. It is my heritage to stand erect, proud and unafraid; to think and act for myself, enjoy the benefit of my creations and to face the world boldly and say, this I have done. All this is what it means to be an American. I do not choose to be common."

Remember that: Greatness comes to those who develop a burning desire to succeed. Success is achieved and maintained by those who try—and keep trying. There is no future in saying it cannot be done. Real success—doing your best—is not in the stars or the luck of the draw. It lies within persistent, daily effort. Concentrate your energies and intensity on the successful completion of your goals."—Dean Alfange, Cornell University-trained scholar and businessman.

We all are at different stages of our lives and careers. We cannot just wish or manufacture success! We must start where we are with what we have and knowing that what we have within us is sufficient to move us to the next level. The quickest way to the top is to start at the bottom. The worst days of those who enjoy what they do are better than the best days of those who do not enjoy what they do.

We should all find something we like to do and make it pay. If you find something you love to do you will never have to work a day in your life. It has been said that competency begins when you begin to enjoy your work. We must learn to do at least one thing so well that it is better than what others do so that is highly likely that we will achieve one of our objectives in life.

We must passionately believe that opportunity knocks often, not just once. We should remember that when we knock on opportunity's door, be sure your bags are packed. We must learn to put forth our best efforts and to always do our best because you will achieve excellence while in the pursuit of perfection. We must resist the urge to give up when times are hard! You can make it if you try! We must avoid indecision and signs of weakness because they are responsible for much of the disappointment and discord in the world today.

REPOSITION YOURSELF

Some experts note that individuals may better understand their current location in life by knowing where they have been. Many people blame their current status of life on external forces. These people believe that you must be in the right place at the right time to succeed in life much like winning the lottery. Success is often the result of our desire to acquire a more productive way of life. It is like playing any sport, the more you practice the better you become! The more proficient you become the more you expect to win when you compete in athletics as well as in life.

We have few opportunities to repeat things or a chance to correct the mistakes we may have made earlier in life. There are life lessons learned even in defeat. There are sometimes extreme consequences we must adjust to. When these times occur we must immediately reposition ourselves for a life of freedom and enrichment. This does not mean spend money to make these problems disappear. We must begin to make mental adjustments that will enable one to reject apathy and become open to a more positive view and expectation of life. One must continuously be aware of how others are impacted by our state of mind.

Our behavior can hurt or help those around us each and every day. 20th century parents must teach their children that smart diligent work will lead to a better quality of life. History notes that many of our parents and grandparents spent their lives in physically demanding manual labor jobs on farms or in cities during the twentieth century agricultural/industrial age when productivity centered on efforts and energies, not strategies and structure. Many researchers conclude that our parents prepared us for a world that was passing them by. The 21st century will place a premium on technology knowledge that requires all global citizens to reposition ourselves for a new way of thinking? We should not reduce our potential for greatness by clinging to outdated ideals and mores of our forefathers.

Maintaining the status quo is equivalent to traditional thinking. A progressive and continuous reassessment of attitudes will assist one when determining whether or not to implement antiquated ideology. The introduction of old ideas does not always lead to desired results. Success in this technologically driven world requires that we consistently update our personal philosophy of life.

Far too many people fail to advance because they stay within their inherited framework of life which was put into place by their parents. Some people manage to acquire a higher standard of living in spite of the numerous struggles in life. These are the individuals who zero in on winning as opposed to surviving. They are successful at focusing their talents and energies on quality of life issues.

Tranquility Within
By Charles Michael Choice

Take a moment and look inside your mind
Remembering a soothing moment embedded within
something time has not erased
An experience, a place, a moment framed!
Something treasured, your mind can't forget
It's crystal clear, it was real,
Irreplaceable!
It's a part of who you are
Your mind travels back to it over and over
It gives you the fuel to go on and helps you
appreciate all the things good in life
The foundation of what defines you the person
something that makes you happy to be alive,
regardless to how difficult your journey has been.
That internal spark, deep in your inner being
that you gravitate back to, that special
moment, or place giving you peace of mind.

LOSE THE BATTLE TO WIN THE WAR

It is rare that any athletic team completes a season without losing at least one game. You can't win them all! So it is with our individual lives. We seek to go undefeated but seldom reach that lofty goal. We have to continuously adjust and reset our efforts to achieve some other degree of excellence. Such is life! It is often reported how great generals understand that you cannot win all of the battles and that you cannot be crushed with occasional defeats. We must become more acquainted and understand the significance of perseverance.

We can and must continue to be life long learners and to refortify ourselves against life's constant barrage of challenges. One must embrace the concept that failing is part of life, and an important part of a successful person's life. Most people committed to fulfilling their true potential are more sensitive to their mistakes than the average person. They do not take their losses and botched experiments personally. Extremely successful people are more sensitive, pay greater attention to detail, and examine things more carefully than the average person.

"The Art of War" by Sun Tzu discussed the intricacies of preparing for battle. This book was first written during the Ming dynasty and is a classic in outlining the science of strategies regarding conflict between men. A comparison between martial arts and the art of healing was made even though they appear to be worlds apart in their meanings. They are actually parallel in many ways such as the beliefs that the less needed the better off you are. The more understanding and knowledge you have about the problem, the more success you will have.

The overriding goal is to have superior knowledge and strategy in order to reduce the possibility of conflict. Sun Tzu's philosophy was to overcome opposition armies without fighting, His desire to accomplish the most by doing the least, is a characteristic stamp of Taoism, the ancient tradition of knowledge that fostered both the healing arts and the martial arts in China. The Taote-Ching, or The Way and Its Power, applies the same strategy to society that Sun Tzu attributes to warriors and armies of ancient times.

Many of Sun Tzu's ideas are not very complex and can easily be applied to everyday life in the 21st century. We must plan to do the most difficult things in the world while they are still easy. We must plan to do the greatest things while they are still small. He attributes this basic philosophy to the success of sages (visionary leaders) who ultimately achieve greatness!

He believed that when you possess a deep reservoir of knowledge it allows one to be aware of danger before danger occurs, to be aware of destruction before destruction occurs and to be aware of calamity before calamity occurs. This deep reservoir of knowledge allows individuals to respond powerfully without burdening the body, to exercise the mind without being used by the mind, to work within the world without being affected by the world, to carry out tasks without being obstructed by tasks.

The warriors of ancient Asia used the Taoist or Zen arts to achieve extreme and profound personal calmness not just in battle. The warriors desired to always achieve that sensitivity needed to respond to life's challenges without hesitation. The warriors conditioned their minds to process the given facts and to typically respond with a rationale plan of action. The book highlighted how successful generals must be able to see what others do not see which is often called brilliance.

Generals must know what others often do not know which is often called genius. Brilliant geniuses typically win and defend in such a way as to be unassailable and they attack in such a way as to be irresistible. The ultimate goal of any successful general is to make conflict altogether unnecessary because of their superior knowledge and battlefield strategies.

The minds of brilliant leaders approach life in military terms. Their quest for excellence requires one to strive to be self disciplined and systematic in continuously thinking out of the box. "The Art of War" by Sun Tzu offered a wealth of knowledge that can be adapted to life in the 21st century. We must be able to use our intellect in converting and transferring lessons learned in ancient history to our present stage of life. We must resist the notion to address life issues with little more than raw emotions. We must become accustomed to seriously considering solutions of prior challenges that may have similarities that we can learn from. We run the risk of repeating past failures if these lessons are not discussed and internalized.

Chapter 8

Creating a Personal Vision

In 1988, the introspective yet stirring song "Man In the Mirror" by the late King of Pop, Michael Jackson encouraged men young and old to stop blaming others for the unrelenting adversity in their life. The lyrics strongly suggested that we should stop blindly following others and begin to make personal decisions that help improve the quality of life for the entire world. This author believes that the positive changes we seek can only be achieved through self reflection of ourselves first and foremost. The song challenges us to look within, to be true to one's own self, to be selfless, to persevere, and to keep the faith as we continue toward our goals in life.

We must be resolute in our pursuit of that vision initially created within our mind. If the mind can conceive it, the body can achieve it has been a popular expression for many years. It highlights the importance of creating individual and personal visions statements. We really do not spend enough time developing long and short term roadmaps for our life. Vision is such a hard thing to define, but it is an essential blueprint for success in this global society that we live in today. It forces us to look in the mirror and visualize and prioritize the dreams we will pursue.

The Wind That Fills Our Sail
By Charles Michael Choice

As we do our best to carry on,
We accept the support we receive that allows us to keep standing!
We keep our balance from the unseen
wind that fills our sail!
Although we cannot see it
we feel the power and strength giving us the will to carry on!
Feeling the loss of our love ones,

is always difficult to bear!
There are no words that can adequately express
the pain we have deep within.
But through faith in God, we endure.
Like a ship crossing turbulent seas, the wind fills our sail,
comforts us through power and grace!
We are able to move forward and learn to live life
with the zest they would want us to have!
We build from the love they had for us,
appreciating the wind that fills our sail!

THE POWER OF VISION

Many philosophers, futurists, and psychiatrist believe that healthy well
adjusted young men have a healthy perspective about their future. They
understand the importance of becoming a visionary. They truly believe that it
is important to think, dream and envision your future. Man must be driven by
the significance of having a goal and purpose in life through being a visionary. The following points are generally considered good advice to follow
when forging a personal mindset for the future.

- Vision is the result of dreams and action.
- You can succeed against all odds if you have a profound vision.
- Young people are profoundly affected by their vision of the future.
- Research shows that successful people exercise extensive control of their
  future.
- We must provide a support structure to reach collective goals Kennesaw
  State University (KSU conference).
- Vision can overcome history and economics.
- Man can only live and flourish by looking into the future.
- Man must have something significant to do in his life.

Most of us have heard of the Starfish story that describes how an older
gentleman was walking along the beach when he encountered a young man at
a distance picking up something and tossing it back into the ocean. The older
gentleman at first thought that the younger man was dancing. The curious older
gentleman wondered what the young man could possibly be doing and asked
him. The young man explained that he was throwing starfish back into the
ocean because if he did not throw the starfish back into the ocean they would
certainly die. The older gentleman sarcastically noted that there are thousands
of starfish on this beach and you cannot possibly make a difference.

The young man never stopped to argue with the older gentleman, he kept on enthusiastically doing what he had made a commitment to do. The young man picked up another starfish and finally answered that he could make a difference with this one and threw the beached starfish back into the ocean. The older gentleman contemplated what had happened and came to two conclusions from this encounter.

1. We have all been given talents to make a difference once we find our purpose in life.
2. We must each find our personal calling and work diligently toward completion.

There are three important points to consider about the starfish story and vision:

1. Vision without action is only a dream.
2. Action without vision is just wasted time.
3. Vision combined with action can lead to significant world changes.

PARADIGM PIONEERS

The term Paradigm Pioneers was coined by experts back in the 1970s. They referred to some people as big dreamers who wanted to change the world for the better. The American pioneers of the 1800s courageously traveled to the West in the belief and hope of a better life for them and their families. They were confronted by untold personal hardships such as lack of food, water, Indian attacks and the pressure to help expand the American western borders. They were also given the opportunity to develop an entirely new structured society.

They traveled westward not knowing how each day would be played out in their lives. These people had a positive vision of their future that eventually led to a big payoff in the end. 21st century Americans must once again be more proficient at anticipating the future. The standard ways of doing business have become obsolete. Our ability to successfully confront and resolve problems is the key to a better life.

Cutting edge people are very comparable to Paradigm Pioneers. These are the individuals willing to take the necessary risk in their quest for a better more fulfilling life. They are part of the initial wave of changes. They take higher risks. There are distinct differences between Pioneers and Settlers. Settlers are the ones who take the safe path. They are the ones who are constantly searching for more reasons to justify doing things differently.

The settler is the low risk taker. Many passive 21st century people are at risk of being obsolete or left behind. They are generally waiting for someone else to guide them and to resolve their issues. They are waiting for a blueprint or map to fall into their hands that will safely guide them to a more meaningful existence.

Pioneers

1. Have an understanding of what the important concepts are.
2. Have the intestinal fortitude to act on what they believe with tenacity and courage.
3. Understand that they were in it for the long haul.
4. Understand that you start slowly and then gain momentum.
5. Rely on intuition and not wishful thinking to come up with cutting edge ideas.

Two Essential Attributes of Paradigm Pioneer

1. Intuition is an essential attribute of Paradigm Pioneers. It is the ability to make good decisions with incomplete information. You will never have enough information to prove that you are heading in the right direction. Intuitive feeling is a gut feeling that you are heading in the right direction.
2. Courage is another essential attribute of Paradigm Pioneers
   a. Courage permits us to actualize your intuition Paradigm Pioneers cut into these long established pathways.
   b. The risk of not staying close to the 'Leading Edge' runs the possibility of being obsolete.
   c. The United States of America has traditionally been a Paradigm Shifter (initiates new products and trends.)

Japan experienced much better success as a Paradigm Pioneer immediately after World War II because they did a better job of moving from a embryonic concept into actual production of popular products. A good example of this is Japan's success with Sharp electronics which originated at Westinghouse USA. There are many other examples where the Japanese capitalized on ideas such as the quartz watch, automobile industry, steel processing and many other practices.

How Do Opportunities Like this Slip Away?

1. The settler's mentality typically puts the emphasis on safety first.
2. They insist on waiting until the official numbers come out before they can fully grasp the problem.

3. Americans should strive for continuous improvement in our lives and organizations every day.
4. We must value to be never satisfied with the status quo.

America must practice 'Total Quality Management and Continuous Improvement' that originated in our country but was perfected in post World War II Japan in the following ways:

1. Get outside the comfort level of your current job and find the pioneer shifters.
2. Break your old rules of past success because they are probably out of date.
3. Develop new reading habits (read in areas you have no expertise in).
4. Be ready for the future but don't let it stop you. The gains will far out weigh your failures!
5. Listen! Listen! Listen!
6. The Paradigm Pioneers operationalize what the Paradigm Shifters start!

"Be Unafraid of Uncharted Territories Discover the Opportunities on the Other Side of the Horizon."

—Author Unknown

"Without vision the people perish."

—Bible

ANTICIPATE THE FUTURE

There are life lessons to be learned from the business world that can be applied to most human interactions. We must learn to peer into the future and to initiate new concepts before they become commonly accepted practices. Vision has become one of the most misunderstood words over the past 25 years. Some interpret vision as the equivalent to outstanding achievement. There are others who view vision as deeply held values that can help to unite a society that galvanizes action.

Some people interpret vision as something external to an organization's existence, something that mobilizes energies from within each of us and pulls out our best efforts. Most experts agree that vision is important but, do not agree on what and how to specifically define it. A set of core values must me identified before they become essential beliefs that are unique to your family or organizations.

These guiding principles demand no external justification but are extremely important to those members inside the organization because they have intrinsic value. Each person or company must determine the values it holds to be sacred. These values remain constant and independent of new fads, competition from others and the current environment. There are no universally accepted right core values that all organizations embrace. One must develop their own ideas to suit their own personal needs.

It has been said by many in the past that "if you do not stand for something, you will fall for anything!" What does your belief system say about you? The poem "The Dash" sums up the importance of carving out a credible reputation. This poem takes place at a funeral of a friend. Funerals typically highlight the date of birth and the date of death. This poem discusses the events that took place between the two dashes. This poem reminisces about the houses, cars, jobs, children and other material things accomplished in this life.

It suggests that all of those possessions are fleeting and temporary. The person really wanted to know what lasting impact his friend had on the lives of others. The friend thought about all the time that we spend on uneventful and unimportant things in our lives. He challenged us to be less quick to anger and to try to be more empathetic to others. He noted that we should show more appreciation of our fellow human beings and to be more loving individuals. We should try to create positive memories whenever possible and to remember that we never have as much time on earth to carve out our personal legacy. We should be mindful that the proverbial clock of life is always ticking!

Chapter 9

Get off the Sidelines
and into the Game

McFadden and Whitehead penned the song "Ain't No Stopping Us Now" in 1979. The lyrics talked about the litany of challenges facing young men at that time and why self confidence and perseverance was needed in overcoming any obstacle. The same advice is applicable for today's 21st century males. We must teach them to be ready to enthusiastically participate in the game called life.

We must teach them how to play, to compete, and to win! Young men must acquire the set of skills it will take to be successful in this extremely competitive global economy. The norms and expectations are very different from those of America's Agricultural and Industrial past. One would not start playing a new athletic game without first studying the rules and preparing yourself to become successful by practicing every day.

You must become proficient at something that is of value to the global society. You must identify then define your skill set. It has been said repeatedly that to become an expert at something, you need to read one book per month on that subject for the next two years. This makes sense when you think about people who are doing cutting edge things in the world and receiving extraordinary recognition and pay for what they know. We must once again become "dispensers of knowledge" and not just consumers of products.

BE READY AT ALL TIMES

The scout oath does an excellent job of preparing young men at an early age to believe in honor, God, and adhere to the scout oath. It also encourages young men to help others and to keep their bodies, minds, and morals at an extremely high level. One of the great ironies of life in America is that on the one hand there are great opportunities, but on the other hand there is formidable competition at home and abroad. You cannot be prepared for every potential event.

You must, however, be ready to dive into the game of life and do the best that you can with the resources that are available. The truth is that we may never always be 100% ready for life's unexpected challenges as we move further into the 21st century. This is not the time to sit passively on the sidelines of this game especially when each one of us is expected to produce and contribute at a high level. A good example of this philosophy can be illustrated in a personal experience that happened to me years ago.

I was on the high school junior varsity basketball team and was suddenly called up to the varsity squad. I was initially just pleased to be on the team until one day the coach directed me to get into the game at a crucial time when the outcome of the contest was very much in doubt. I had to make a split second choice to mentally and physically get into the game and do the best I could or to just be pleased to be involved in the action and shuffle through the motions until the contest ended. I chose to play as hard and as smart as I knew how and fortunately I played a key role in our team winning over a more dominant opponent.

I often wonder what my life would be like if I had displayed a frightened, nonchalant, or complacent attitude and had not made a significant contribution in our winning effort. As it turned out, my reputation had been established as someone who could be counted on in difficult times. Someone who played the game the right way! Someone who would not quit in the face of seemingly insurmountable odds! My reputation had been forged during a critical time in my life.

This author can recall a second personal story that led to another significant boost in my career. I had just moved from Ohio to the state of Georgia in 1991, from principal in a relatively small school system to one of the largest systems in the Southeastern part of the United States. I was originally disappointed when I had to accept my new assignment as assistant principal at one of the many high schools in Cobb County Georgia. I did not complain! I simply went about my job and performed the best that I could. I was more than a little disappointed when I remained in the same assistant principalship assignment going into my second year in Georgia.

I continued to carry myself in the most professional way that I knew and it paid off when I got an unexpected phone call from the Cobb County Board of Education officials in late September 1992. I was instructed to report to Central Office at 7:00 p.m. on Tuesday evening. They did not tell me why. They just said to report on time! I had to be ready for anything, both the good and the bad!

I was immediately met by three of the Cobb County School District Associate Superintendents of this prestigious school system. To say that I was a little concerned is an understatement! My first response was to ask them if I was in trouble. They informed me that I was not but, that they had a tremendous opportunity that they wanted me to consider. They explained that they needed a seasoned administrator to become the next principal of Wheeler High School.

They proceeded to tell me about the schools' excellent reputation, the award winning students, ultra successful athletic teams as well as the outstanding parental support, and involvement. They must have gone on extolling the virtues of this fine educational institution for the next 20 minutes. They then asked me if I was ready and willing to accept this new challenge. I said that I was eager to get started but, I wanted a few days to digest the information they had shared with me during the last 35 minutes.

I had been prepared to make an orderly transition at the end of the first semester. They told me that this offer would only be on the table for the next 10 minutes. They expected me to report first thing the next morning to my new assignment. I was flabbergasted at the swiftness of this immediate change in assignment. I presented more than half a dozen excuses for delaying the move. Finally, the exasperated associate superintendents began to wonder if I was truly the right man for the job and one of them asked me point blank if I really wanted this job. I answered in the affirmative. Yes, I wanted this job, starting tomorrow, but I did have one last question. Where was Wheeler High School? I had been so busy and so new to Cobb County that I had no idea where this school was actually located.

I reported to my new school the next morning and stayed for five outstanding years. My claim to fame was leading our school in the improvement of our SAT (Scholastic Aptitude Test) scores by 43 points in three years. We initiated several new student focused, rigorous, academic programs that generated a reputation of providing cutting edge ideas and concepts with a diverse population of students in the 'Deep South.'

What the associate superintendents failed to explain to me is that I would be the first ever African American high school principal in this growing, ultra conservative county. The success Wheeler High School experienced was enjoyed by students, faculty, staff as well as our community. I again, often wonder what would have become of me if I had rejected the offer to immediately become the principal with only a few hours notice. Thankfully, I had been ready to not only get into the game but, to perform and win under pressure. That daunting experience made a lasting and significant impact on the direction and the number of options that have been presented to me during the remainder of my professional career. This was the perfect storm when opportunity met preparation!

Winners and Losers
Unknown Author

The Winner is always part of the answer
The Loser always part of the problem
The winner always has a program
The Loser always has an excuse
The Winner says, "Let me do it for you";
The Loser says, "That's not my job,"
The Winner sees an answer for every problem;
The Loser sees a problem for every answer.
The Winner sees a green near every sand trap;
The Loser sees two or three sand traps near every green.
The Winner says, "It may be difficult but it's possible"
The Loser says, "It may be possible but it's too difficult."
"Knowing where you're going is the first step to getting there."

We desperately need to transition America's educational philosophy from old stale 20th century top down leadership styles to a more optimistic 21st century model. The old hitching post should be used to tie down horses not used as a guidepost. The Tyranny of Dead Ideas book offers some intriguing advice for us to consider. We personally know the power that dead ideas have had on our lives and how hard it is to break free from their unrelenting grip. We learned in childhood some of those old dead ideas and yet they still define who we are as adults.

People and organizations are teetering on extinction simply because they cannot begin to think out of the box during the 21st century. They would rather hold on to tired old ideas because this is the way they have always done things. This of course, makes no sense! Americans seek certainty, consistency, and continuity in an environment that seems to be changing as we speak. It is no longer in our best interest to hold tight to outdated beliefs and traditions. It is counterproductive to realizing our nation's true potential.

Many of these ancient ideas have become dangerous and counterproductive. Americans cannot afford to impose limitations on our minds at exactly the moment when new ways of interpreting and processing data are needed. There will be an abundance of opportunities that will require people who embrace cutting edge thinking. The sky is the limit if you prepare yourself to dare to be great and have little fear of the unknown. Great leaders often develop during times of crisis. These are the individuals who can hit the ground running and are not afraid of failure.

There are a number of qualities that most capable leaders possess. The following concepts are essentials skills that all leaders seem to display.

1. A leader illustrates a strong curiosity about life. He will listen to people outside of the inner circle crowd. He reads consistently, because the world is a big, complicated place. If a leader never steps outside his comfort zone to hear different ideas, he grows stale.
2. A leader has to be willing to create new ways of doing things. They must be willing to go out on a limb, and be willing to try something different. Leadership is all about managing change. Things change, and you must become creative. You learn how to adapt to life's changes.
3. A leader must possess exceptional communication skills. This does not mean limited to oratory abilities. They must face reality and always tell the truth.
4. A leader must display character that is always on display. That means knowing the difference between right and wrong and having the moral compass to do the right thing.
5. A leader must be courageous. Tough talk is not courage. Courage in the 21st century doesn't mean posturing and bravado. Courage is a commitment to sit down at the negotiating table and talk.
6. A leader must have strong convictions and a passion to accomplish what you set out to do. You must have a strong desire to really get something done.
7. A leader should have charisma. The quality that makes people choose to follow you. The ability to inspire people to follow a leader because they trust him.
8. A leader must be competent in order to have any credibility with his troops. You must know what you're doing. More important than that, you've got to surround yourself with people who know what they are doing.
9. A leader must have common sense. Human beings have the ability to reason and use their intellect to resolve simple and complex problems.

We need inspirational leaders who value community first and self second. These are the individuals who seem to be in the right place at the right time. They get a great deal of personal satisfaction when performing difficult tasks on behalf of others. These are the people who always seem busy and often have more than one iron in the fire. Their plate is always full and yet they seldom shy away from additional substantive challenges. How do these individuals stay so positive, even when things do not always workout perfectly for them? How does one remain motivated in spite of overwhelming odds?

How do supposedly inferior athletic teams manage to come away with championship trophies long after the so called experts dismissed their chances? Many of the answers can be attributed to self confidence and thorough preparation. Self Motivation and continuous improvement are topics that need to be further addressed as we approach the second decade of the 21st century. We need to better understand ourselves and know how to effectively work with an increasingly diverse global population.

Several experts have generated current research on human achievement. They identified three motivational categories. Understanding what drives us, what is needed to be motivated, and what rewards are effective and helpful to accomplishing and maintaining focus on goals. The following summations can help us learn more about our leadership styles:

The Producer is the classic 'Type A' and has self-discipline, is competitive, and decisive. You can be considered a producer if you are driven by competition and deadlines. You are a connector if you value relationships, teamwork and collaboration over anything else. Connectors put relationships first and are loyal, supportive, team players. They find satisfaction in making others happy.

The stabilizer is careful, analytic, practical and sometimes comfortable with the status quo. They value order and predictability. Stabilizers seek to reduce distractions and use rules to make their positions palatable with their constituents. What inspires you to do your best? You have an internal focus if you desire to be appreciated for your contribution. You find satisfaction from meaningful work and need to feel good about what they are doing.

Internal focuses maintain motivation with positive feedback and goals they find meaningful. They seek to find ways to see the overall big picture when signs of motivation are not evident. External focuses are success-oriented and value tangible assets to measure success. They can maintain motivation by celebrating achievements with incremental improvement. Effective leaders should seek to identify their individual style and the styles of their constituents in or to properly inspire and motivate.

Trust is essential to every individual, economy, nation, and civilization in the world. Once trust is removed it has the potential to destroy the most powerful government, the most successful business, the most influential leadership, the most expansive economy, the greatest friendship, the strongest character, and the deepest love. When trust is introduced and leveraged properly, it has the potential to generate unimaginable success and prosperity. Trust adds new dimensions to individuals and to the spontaneity of an organization. The importance of trust is often neglected and always underestimated.

Trust impacts our lives every day of the year. It determines the quality of life of every community, every relationship, every business venture, and every effort we initiate with other individuals. Trust is a tangible asset that is hard to develop but, easy to destroy and even harder to replace. Some suggest that the absence of trust is one of the greatest issues facing young men today as they transition from adolescence to the adult world? It's as though America's adults have collectively lost confidence in young men and vice versa. Far too many 21st century young men no longer believe, fear, or respect many of the traditional role models that older adults hold dearly. A much larger question is, once lost, how does one generation earn back that powerful concept called trust.

Trust means confidence and distrust leads to suspicion. When you trust people, you have confidence in them and believe in their abilities and integrity. When you distrust people, you are suspicious of them and of their agenda, their capabilities, and their history. We all know the value of establishing rock solid relationships that emanate from trust on both sides. The results can be extraordinary once these once competing differences can be reconciled.

Could it be that many young men do not trust adults because they don't want to, once again, be disappointed or abandoned? Far too many adults have demonstrated a propensity for disappearing from the lives of 21st century young men at their most critical developmental stages. Can we ever begin to earn back their trust? Many parents and guardians have entrusted America's children to be nurtured, educated and reared by strangers who happen to work in our public schools. These underperforming and poorly prepared paycheck educators along with overwhelmed social agencies, and the maligned juvenile justice departments have contributed to students performing significantly below their capacity. Much of the blame can be laid at the doorstep of public schools' over-reliance on dated practices that no longer connect with 21st century students.

America's rapidly growing social agencies, systems, and organizations are little more than job entitlement programs for adults. We are warehousing our most vulnerable children at critical junctions in their lives where there is little hope for independence or self improvement once kids are in the clutches of many of these programs. We must radically implement and improved our systems thinking approaches that puts into place significant rewards for professionals who assist young people in reaching their true potential. We must reassert our role as the caring, yet demanding adult figure in the lives of America's children. Lowering the bar is no longer a viable feel good option for our young men if we are truly committed to the long term success of our nation.

Chapter 10

Huddle-Up

The 1996, song "I Believe I Can Fly" by R. Kelly speaks about the importance of believing in oneself. It starts with a strong abiding belief in our own innate abilities. It really does not matter how others see you. It is more important how you view yourself! Most things are truly attainable and are within your grasps. Boys must stop settling for low hanging fruit that requires less effort to attain. Reach for the moon and if you fall among the stars you are still in a more lofty position from where you started. That deceptive swagger that is all too apparent in many young men is nothing more than hiding their inadequacies.

We must systematically teach our young men how to intellectually soar like eagles once again. Their bravado often masks their intellectual insecurities which lie deep within far too many 21st century males. You must believe you are intellectually capable of outstanding performances before it can ever come to fruition. Individuals and teams rise to mythical standards of excellence once there is individual and collective "buy-in" of the high expectations set before them. Individual teams must display that quiet, genuine self confidence at all times when facing insurmountable odds. Individuals and teams must strive for excellence in everything that they do! The development of self confidence is similar to athletics in that the more you practice, the better you become.

You do not become a very good athlete without consistent practice, hard work and self sacrifice to reach your goals. A similar analogy can be made for just about any worthwhile milestone in life once we believe that we have the wherewithal to complete that task. We cannot be afraid of failure!

Every day, in every way, I am getting better and better.
I begin each day with a positive mental attitude (PMA).
I will not allow anyone or anything to steal my joy.
I am happy. I am healthy. I am hopeful.
I am in control of my mind, my body and my life.
I have the power to be happy, positive and successful.
I can achieve my dream with high self-esteem.
I am smart. I am special. I am somebody!
I can be anything that I want to be, if I put my mind to it.
I have the desire, discipline and determination to be the best
I am bold. I am brave. I am beautiful. I am one of a kind.
I know that the real key to success is to care enough to do my best.

—Mike Howard, Motivational Speaker

The following is a wonderful poem that we all should eternalize.

"Tis a lesson you should heed, try, try again; If at first you don't succeed, try, try again; Then your courage should appear, for, if you will persevere, you will conquer, never fear; try, try again."

—Author Unknown

This prose is even more important today as we continue to experience a revolution of new technology and ideas during the early part of the 21st century. The proliferation of new trends, products, concepts and attitudes seem to be changing at warp speed. Those who are slow to make adjustments are relegated to permanent catch up status. One must ride the crest of change or risk being sucked underneath the unforgiving waves. It is as if nothing is sacred or permanent anymore. We must collectively resist the notion that many young men are destined to be part of a sinister planned obsolescent point of view.

There are those who believe that the American society has been too strongly influenced by consumerism which has had a dramatically negative impact on the psyche of how we see many young boys. There are still others who believe that it is in our nation's best interest to treat some young men as disposal items that can be easily replaced. These people highlight the following examples: throwaway diapers, disposable plastic spoons, knives, forks, toilet tissue, cotton swabs and pads, shaving razors, toothbrushes, hospital aprons, medical and cleaning gloves, paper and plastic shopping bags, overflowing landfills, temporary foster families, a temporary job picture, and fragile, temporary relationships.

What is really permanent anymore? Nothing ever seems to last or remain the same from day to day, week to week, or year to year. Some of these changes are positive and yet untold other changes negatively impact one's mental or physical quality of life. It is time for all well intentioned Americans to regroup and determine what we want to see our young men accomplish in life. We must once again make an effort to capitalize on our nation's love affair with athletics and to utilize that most familiar refrain that is understood by all participants.

Huddle-Up! This term is drilled into the subconscious of all athletes, coaches, parents, and spectators from a very early age until the day they retire from active involvement. The symbolic meaning is a command to come together as a kindred group to hear new directives for the next course of action. When the term Huddle-Up is uttered, it means that everyone on the athletic field of play must immediately stop what they are doing, regroup, and ready themselves for new instructions.

Disciplined organized teams do not stop to argue about recently missed assignments but instead, but instead, make well thought out short term adjustments. Participants don't give half hearted efforts even if they do not agree 100% with the new strategy. They do not second guess the instructions being directed by the leaders on and off the field. Everyone has their individual assignments and is expected to carry them out to the best of their abilities or risk being replaced by someone else on the team. To Huddle-Up allows a team to collect their thoughts, catch their breath, and begin to concentrate on the next short term mission.

The best coaches understand that they will need to change or update strategies numerous times during the course of the game if their ultimate goal remains to win the overall battle. There will be a number of instances when the original game plan must be dramatically changed. To Huddle-Up does not indicate failure, but simply a course adjustment. This contrasts sharply to what currently takes place in our schools, our homes, and our communities. It is as though adults never feel empowered to Huddle-Up, to be able to deliberately plan and develop a different, more relevant set of strategies for the more immediate challenges facing boys. There now seems to be an absence of current, well thought out directions while fighting this enormously complicated battle for the lives and souls of 21st century young men. It is as though the flawed blueprint for raising young men that is currently in place must suffice for lack of effort, ingenuity, or a national commitment.

Can America really afford to write off such a large portion of our society? This author believes that this war on behalf of young men can and will be won when we decide to attack the problem with a nationwide, systematic and disciplined approach. Americans must merely review negative 21st century trend data regarding our young men to conclude that radical new strategies must immediately be implemented. The majority of mid 20th century America relied on what many people referred to as a 'Triad" or three legged stool' to provide a consistent forum for resolving and discussing community concerns of the day. The following entities were considered equal partners:

1. The home
2. The school
3. The church/community

These bastions of stability offered three opportunities for stakeholders to come together to address some of the life defining issues that were seen as having significant impact on young people. This three legged stool or 'Triad' always seemed to be in sync with each other and their roles were clearly defined. As we experience the revolution that is called global living, many of these past traditional norms are in disrepair or under tremendous assault. We, therefore, must develop systematic, wholesome new traditions to replace these lost or damaged tenets.

Many young men believe that with the elimination of the three legged stool that nothing is actually very permanent in their lives anymore. Many young men live their life only for today! It is said that far too many young men do not believe that they will live to be twenty five years old. Many young men are looking for something to hold onto and to realistically believe in. This has led far too many young men to make a series of very bad, self destructive decisions. The three legged Triad provided an oasis of stability and calmness during most of the 20th century.

It has been under siege for the past forty years and currently offers little solace and peace of mind. Many young men are left to grasp meaningless ideas and fads that offer little more than a temporary diversion from the sad state of affairs that now describes the harsh times they call life. Young men, in particular, seem to be at a loss when defining who they are, what they stand for, and how they view themselves. It is up to America's wise and caring 'Elders' to assist in providing these young men with role models, positive images, and healthy options to emulate.

Adults must prepare America's young men not to just survive, but to flourish in these increasingly complicated and difficult times. Young men should not be seen as disposable items but, as essential building blocks to the successful foundation of our nation's future. This, of course, is a monumental task that requires careful planning and forethought. It is this author's belief that we should begin by teaching the 'Intangibles of Life.' Once these beliefs are mastered they can be tailored to fit most individuals as well as the environment from which they currently reside. The Intangibles are those abstract terms and themes that rarely change from the cradle to the grave. The following graphic is indicative of the representation of the basic "Intangibles of Life."

INTANGIBLES OF LIFE

1. Responsibility: mental accountability
2. Self Discipline: training that corrects molds or perfects mental faculties or moral character.

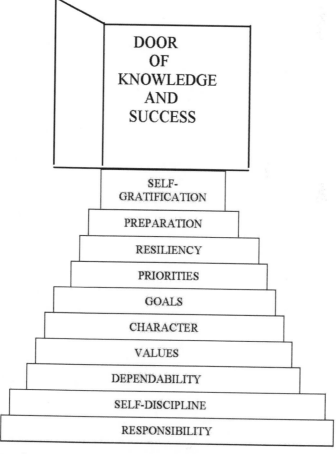

Graph 10.1. Door Of Knowledge And Success

3. Dependability: to place reliance or trust in something or someone.
4. Values: beliefs those are intrinsically important or desirable to you.
5. Character: the aggregate of distinctive moral qualities that an individual possesses. The attributes or features that make up and distinguish an individual from another.
6. Goals: the end results toward directed personal efforts
7. Priorities: the preferential rating of internal efforts.
8. Resiliency: the ability to recover quickly from adverse change or misfortune.
9. Preparation: the process of making something ready for execution of the end result.
10. Self Gratification: a source of personal satisfaction and individual achievement.

What is it about these 'Intangibles of Life' that make them just as important today as they were 100 years ago? These concepts all center on human development and interaction. They are flexible enough to apply to most cultures and they have been able to sustain the test of time.

The following questions must still be raised regarding these intangibles.

1. Why these intangibles are important in today's technologically advanced world?
2. Why do some individuals, families, schools, and organizations appear more successful in achieving these intangibles than others?
3. What is the best way to teach individuals the importance of these themes?
4. How have these intangibles managed to survive the onslaught of radical 21st century changes?

It is the belief of this author that many adults have failed to pass along important information (Oral Traditions) to young men that is essential for living healthy, intellectually inspiring, independent lives. There must be a consistent drumbeat of encouragement when interacting with today's young men. There has been an absence of systematic, well thought out support systems that must to be corrected immediately. America is in a critical battle for the hearts and minds of our country' young men and therefore needs to adjust its direction immediately. These are street smart kids whose energy should be channeled into more wholesome, realistic end products. We must be prepared to earn their trust.

We must individually work and teach young men that life enhancing, healthy options are available if they follow a clear, well thought out plan.

Work smarter, not harder! No pain, no gain! It is counterproductive for adults to use their power over children in an attempt to intimidate and control our youth. Adults must demonstrate the power of love, concern and kindness! Young men must be passionately encouraged (tough love) the way we would cheer on our favorite athletic hero and team.

You Are the Best
Author Unknown

Don't follow the crowd and try to be like all of the rest.
Remember that you are the best.
so when you get tired and want to stop
keep on going until you reach the top.
Believe in yourself and don't hesitate
to let others know that you are great
Expand your mind and continue to grow,
for you will always be the star of the show.
Strive to achieve excellence in all that you do
for God knew what he was doing when he created you.
Think before you act, work on before you rest,
and let the world know that you are the Best.

LAWS OF ATTRACTION

America must take personal inventory and stock to determine what is really important in our lives. We can begin by making a list of the things we are thankful and grateful for. It offers a number of common sense ideas that are embraced by many successful individuals. It offers the following basic concepts that lead to a better understanding and appreciation of us. We must all take time for self reflection to confirm those things that we value most in our lives. The following ideas are suggested:

Gratitude Leads to Attitude

We should close our eyes everyday and quietly visualize our dreams.
We must commit ourselves to act when we have inspired thoughts.
We need to declare and pursue those spelled out personal goals in life.
We must not focus on the lack or scarcity of a given product or ideas because you then begin to attract what you do not have.
We must focus what you desire out of life. We must pursue the inner joys first and the outer tangible joys will follow.
Every wish we think will manifest itself.

Relationships

You must enjoy yourself first before others enjoy you

You must treat yourself the way you want others to treat you.

A healthy respect for you is ok

Write down all the things you appreciate about your life, (people and organizations)

We create our own happiness.

Only one person can be in charge of your joy and happiness.

Do not give anyone else permission to make decisions about my life.

Your joy lies within you.

Do not let others steal your joy.

Placebo stories note that the mind is the greatest factor in many health illustrations.

Happier thoughts lead to happier physiological results.

You can put things back together again in your mind.

Nothing should distract you from your goals and vision in life.

Man becomes what he thinks about.

We sometimes become content with thing that we do not want.

We sometimes add our energy to negative things (drugs, poverty, and racial injustice).

What you resist will often persist.

We need to focus on what you want to see as the outcome

Anti war evolves into pro peace

Anti poverty evolves into pro prosperity

Anti hunger evolves into pro healthy diet

Anti dropout evolves into pro quality education

Energy flows where attention goes.

There is more than enough to go around.

There is more than enough joy, creativity, power, and wealth.

We must open up our vision.

You must become intentional and be on fire.

Empowering and sharing with others is at our finger tips.

All power is within.

When you focus on what you want, what you do not want falls away.

Break away from hereditary patterns, and cultural norms

Whether you think you can or you think you cannot. You are right either way!

Your mission is the mission you give yourself.

When you follow your bliss, it becomes contagious.

A future of unbounded talent is reduced because we are only using 5% of the human mind

You were born to add value to your life and your job.

How well you seize the moment will determine whether you master the secrets of life.

CHAMPIONSHIP COACHING FOR LIFE

Coaching is about inspiring the best athletic performance out of your student athletes. The most successful coaches encourage young men to make good decisions that will improve the quality of their life on and off the field. Successful coaches are concerned about improving student relationships with teammates, teachers, family and the community. The most revered coach is as concerned with his student's learning the lessons in life as much as they are concerned with teaching the Xs and Os of winning games. They generally consider athletic coaching and coaching for life as interchangeable. The goal of each is to bring out the best of the individuals they work with.

The good coach helps his players better understand themselves. The excellent coaches continuously discover new things about themselves as well as his student athletes. Great coaches understand it is not about them! They enjoy molding and shaping teams to bring out the best talents in their athletes. The great coach must always demonstrate resourcefulness and know how to snatch that winning spirit from the jaws of defeat.

The following are important skills that championship coaches adhere to:

1. Championship coaches know that listening is more important that talking. Most young people overcome their fear and distrust of adults when they are given an adult's undivided attention. This often leads to questioning and self reflection.
2. Championship coaches understand the value of effective communication skills. They are able to interpret and better understand their players with fewer prejudge mental responses.
3. Championship coaches have the ability to build rapport with the vast majority of young people. The successful coach is able to concentrate on one individual at a time. This helps to build rapport between coach and athlete.
4. Championship coaches know how to motivate their players and are constantly ready to help their players improve. A personal relationship must be established with a young person before success can be realized.
5. Championship coaches understand the importance of treating everyone uniquely different. Human emotions and personal feelings are extremely important. They believe that all students can be successful if they are willing to embrace team goals first.

PRINCIPLES OF SUCCESSFUL COACHING FOR LIFE

1. Listen thoroughly before talking
2. Know what the motivation is for each of your players
3. Every young person has the potential to grow and achieve something.
4. The past reputation of a person should not determine his future success
5. Encourage your players to dream big
6. Be supportive at all times.
7. Encourage self discovery and self reflection
8. Reduce negative criticism
9. Use discretion when dealing with personal student exchanges
10. Team success trumps individual recognition

Effective coaches know how to capture the imagination of their 21st century athletes. The following is an account of a down to earth approach implemented by a highly successful football coach who managed to help his athlete's transition from the playing field to the much more rigorous lessons of life. It is the responsibility of adults to create environments that are proactive with an expectation to do the right thing. Effective coaches must help create a nurturing culture and supportive community. Adults must provide young people with realistic experiences as well as create positive memories that encourage respect and dignity toward others. These community building ideas were designed to promote lifelong benefits and to reduce those behaviors that harm or demean other individuals.

Coach Joe Ehrmann, a former National Football League player, founded a community center known as The Door while serving as an inner-city minister. He co-founded a Ronald McDonald House for seriously ill children and their families. This project helped to promote racial harmony in the Baltimore, Maryland community. He developed very insightful observations, especially related to the psychological development of boys.

Coach Ehrmann strongly believed that too many young men were brought up to believe in what he termed false masculinity. This was described as judging success in terms of athletic ability, sexual conquest, and economic success. He believed that males spend far too much time comparing and competing. This results in men feeling isolated and alone. The term false masculinity has been a part of the macho world of young men for the past fifty years.

This championship coach advocated the creation of a new definition of what it means to be a man and he labeled it strategic masculinity. It emphasized building nurturing relationships with others and identifying and working for a cause beyond oneself. 21st century males must somehow understand that masculinity must be defined by its capacity to love and to be loved. The following questions should be asked when determining ones general claim to being a real man.

1. What kind of son are you?
2. What kind of teammate are you?
3. What kind of coach or husband are you?
4. What kind of father are you?
5. What kind of friend are you?

Success comes from developing healthy, consistent relationships. Man must have some purpose and cause in his life that is bigger that our own personal hopes, personal dreams and selfish desires. When we transition toward the end of our life we should have tangible evidence that we were more concerned about the wellbeing and welfare of others rather than for our own personal gain. We must be willing to share this updated philosophy on what it means to be a man to young men all over America. Athletics is about living in a community and developing nurturing relationships in which each player serves to enhance the lives of others.

We must consistently emphasized concepts such as empathy, inclusion, and honesty. Many 21st century student athletes initially are reluctant, and embarrassed to accept these new belief systems. There is however, 100% buy in once they are around older players who genuinely care about them. This helped to create a more nurturing and supportive group of young men who respected and affirmed each other.

The following coaching philosophy is embraced by a number of successful coaches:

1. Do not dismiss a player from the team based solely on athletic ability.
2. Play seniors each game regardless of the score of a game.
3. Encourage and build up players and never humiliate or demean.
4. Eliminate sarcasm when correcting young men.

Many championship coaches regularly encourage their senior players to become more reflective about their personal lives. They are asked to openly share the impact they have made on their community. Each senior will address his teammates at the end of the season, prior to the last game. Many championship coaches expect their student athletes to read a personal essay titled, "How I want to Be Remembered When I Die." This exercise has resulted in many young men taking a much closer look into their future and envisioning what community impact they wanted to make about their lives before they died.

Many championship coaches focus on emphasizing the lifelong lessons of respecting oneself and others, being empathetic and contributing to the welfare of others. These ideas were far more important components in life than the outcome of a football game! The goal of any credible coach is for young men to understand that defeat on the football field was tolerable as long as players consistently displayed caring and compassion for their fellow man on and off the field.

KEEP THE END IN MIND

What is it that we want to see in our young men? Is it a change in the style of clothing that has evolved so radically over the past few years? Is it their value system that unfortunately often praises the misogynistic ramblings of today's pop culture? Is it their redefining and interpretation of the 21st century family? What is the final product that we desire to see in young men everywhere throughout the United States of America? We can no longer postpone or avoid addressing these issues in the hope that they will resolve themselves any time soon. We must address these questions and implement exciting, comprehensive strategies if America is to realize its ongoing mission of creating healthy, well adjusted young men who successfully transition into strong heads of households in the years to come.

This book has primarily focused on the shortcomings of young men. Upon closer reflection, the real challenge should be how responsible caring adults provide leadership, empathy and understanding of the psychological needs of young 21st century males. It all goes back to one of Stephen Covey's, "Seven Habits of Highly Effective People." One of his chapters is titled "Seek First To Understand, Then to be Understood." This is exactly the advice that Americans need to follow.

Adult assistance and intervention is required in a profound and systematic way. Our young men must be made to feel valued and connected to someone or something. We must no longer fear them or marginalize their intellectual competencies in order to celebrate their more heralded athletic prowess. Far too many adults have discounted the academic potential of young men to the extent that it has permanently limited their quality of life options. We must be much more deliberate, strategic and consistent when interacting with America's 21st century young men. Adults must be more responsible for modeling through words and deed the message of respect and love. This message must be emphasized daily by all adults who are privileged to interact with America's young men.

Low Cost Interactions Adults Must Promote With Young Men That Are Deemed Valuable:

1. Adults must be proactive in creating environments in which children resist demeaning others not because they fear punishment but, because they know it is the wrong thing to do.
2. Adults must provide youth with realistic messages and memorable activities that encourage respect and dignity towards oneself and others. The more we allow youngsters to experience the joys and benefits of pro social behaviors, the less likely they are to exhibit behaviors that harm others.
3. Adults must understand that many young men are conditioned to believe in false masculinity where success is based upon athletic ability, sexual conquest, and economic success. Too much male competition leaves men feeling isolated, alone and destroys any concept of community.
4. Adults must acknowledge a new definition of what it means to be a 21st century man and label it strategic masculinity. It emphasizes nurturing relationships with others as well as working for a cause beyond oneself.
5. Adults need to understand the value of showing ownership for the success of some kind of cause, some kind of purpose in our lives that is bigger than our own individual hopes, dreams, wants and desires. What legacy do you want to leave?
6. Adults should insist that players have a servant attitude and always be willing to assist others.
7. Adults should model lifelong lessons of respecting oneself and others, being empathetic and contributing to the welfare of others are far more important than the outcome of a game.
8. Adults have the responsibility for incorporating respect and love into our interactions with children and adolescent on a daily basis.

Stinging Words Cause Heart Pains
By Charles Michael Choice

When the tongue lashes out unkind words the
heart absorbs a direct hit!
The recipient cannot avoid the sustained pain!
Lovers quarrels where verbal blows go back and forth,
can do more damage than hardened fists!
Vicious statements in the heat of battle can
never be erased from one's mind!
Perhaps in time they can be forgiven,
but never forgotten!
It is a contest to see who can get in the last verbal jab!

Words are powerful and have an everlasting effect!
They are used as weapons,
inflicting much pain!
Think carefully before going on an all out assault.
Choose your words wisely.
Don't lose the love of your life
because of an uncontrollable vicious tongue!

REPAIRING THE WOUNDED HUMAN SPIRIT

It is this author's assertion that many 21st century young men suffer from a wounded or broken spirit. A wounded or broken spirit is defined as one that is hurting, but also one in which the hurt has festered into negative attitudes and responses. A person with a wounded spirit lives in self imposed misery that focuses regularly on his personal suffering. The following are unbearable wounded spirit characteristics:

1. A negative mind-set. The person with a wounded spirit is preoccupied with past injuries. He views incidents in life in the worst possible way. He sees the bad and ignores the good. His mind is an accumulation of negative thoughts. A person with a wounded spirit views himself as a victim who constantly sufferers. He is satisfied when others notice his misery, and hurt when they do not.
2. A person with a wounded spirit holds other people responsible for the misery in his life. He is quick to blame others. He is quick to blame others for his plight in life. Fate is ultimately in control of his destiny.

It is the observation of this author that there appears to be an all out assault on the part of large numbers of adults to rob many of America's young men of one of their truly unique attributes. I am referring to the beautiful, boundless, positive human spirit children often leave home with each day. You may ask how this is possible or why would any rational adult deliberately set upon this course of action? The following are my own personal thoughts regarding this subject.

We know that robbery and theft are considered crimes, and yet thousands of young men all across our great nation are systematically being separated from the very essence of their being. What is this 'Human Spirit' I am alluding to and how and why is such a callused act tolerated? Why do some young men seem to have an abundance of this very intangible substance while many others appear listless and devoid of any real zest for life? Caring adults must redefine its role and responsibility to young men for repairing their fragile human wounded spirits.

There is a litany of problems that public schools across America need to address before a consistently high quality education and prospects of a brighter future can be achieved by all students. You have all heard about school related concerns regarding unruly students, deficiencies in the buildings, inadequate supplies, outdated textbooks, single parent families, diminishing tax bases, shortage of visionary leaders, low expectations, apathetic business communities, unwed mothers, increased gang activities, unequal distribution of resources, and unprepared and uncaring paycheck teachers. The list could go on and on.

This author has come to several basic realizations after studying some of these issues regarding how male students respond to adult interactions throughout the United States. The following are themes that I believe are essentially true regarding 21st century school aged young men.

THINGS I HAVE LEARNED ABOUT YOUNG MEN

- I have learned that you cannot make young men love you,
  All you can do is carry yourself in a way that promotes mutual respect.
- I have learned that no matter how much young men care,
  Some significant adults refuse to show affection and concern in return.
- I have learned that it takes years to build up trust with many young men,.
  And only seconds to destroy it with a harsh word or negative body language.
- I have learned that it is not what a young man has in his life,
  but who a young man has in his life that counts.
- I have learned that many young men will try to initially get by on charm or swagger,
  After that, they need to know that intelligence will get them further ahead in life.
- I have learned that young men will do testosterone driven irrational things in an instant,
  That will give them heartaches for a lifetime.
- I have learned that young men can keep going physically and emotionally,
  Long after others have told them that the odds are stacked against them and success appears far too hopeless.
- I have learned that young men must be held responsible for their actions,
  This is called 'Tough Love' no matter how angry or emotional they might feel.

- I have learned that young men must be responsible for controlling their own attitude and destiny or they will be left with few options in life and no viable future.
- I have learned that sometimes the people you expect to kick young men when they are down will actually be the first ones to help them get back up.
- I have learned that young men must learn how to trust again!
- I have learned that adults should never tell young men their dreams are unlikely or outlandish, It is much nobler to assist them in envisioning a limitless future.
- I have learned that a young man's background and circumstances may have influenced who they are today, but young men are primarily responsible for determining their own future.
- I have learned that even when you think young men have no earthly things to give,young men will somehow find the resources, resolve and resilience to assist when a friend needs their help.

Many adults give considerable attention and attach significant importance to caring for the body (eat, sleep, exercise, clothes, medicine) and toward nurturing and cultivating the soul (education, career, friends, entertainment) but provide little interest and insight into the development of the human spirit. The human spirit in many of our 21st century young men is essentially latent (yet to be discovered) rather than actualized (being used), and this results in unrealized potential for many of America's children. 21st century young men come to school in all sizes, shapes, colors, and conditions in their lives. It should not be the mission of adults to further condemn, admonish, ridicule, or to withhold information because we disagree with their lifestyle or find repugnant the sometimes harsh hand many male students have been dealt in their short life span.

This must be our time to replenish, to renew, to reenergize, to restore, to rekindle, to rehabilitate, and to recommit to the very students we are expected to teach and nurture. How does one go about repairing the human spirit? We understand the repair of things tangible but know little about the fragile human spirit. Many tangible things can be kept for personal use. If you have a new car, suit or shirt, you might keep it for yourself. Things of the spirit cannot be kept like possessions. Love and genuine concern for others is not something to be put in a closet, stored away and never to be shared.

You run the risk of those items becoming impotent, lifeless or unusable when left too long in a dormant state. One must put things of the spirit into action. One must share the beacon of the spirit with others in order to create meaning. It is too important to simply put on a shelf because it all too soon becomes out of date. Educators and other concerned adults cannot walk the path of the spirit and be a person who cares for no one but themselves.

The kind of person who lives his own life in solitary and gives nothing he has to anyone. This type of teacher cannot awaken the spirit within 21st century students. To awaken the spirit within them one must learn to care for others, to love others, to share the wealth of their knowledge of the spirit of their heart with others, so that those students might once again experience the joys of learning. Children must once again possess that spirit of success! This is the kind of spirit that will not allow anyone to stand in the way of their goals.

This is the kind of spirit that will not allow anyone to defer their dreams. This is the kind of spirit that will not allow anyone to stifle the creative dreams of young men. This is the kind of spirit that will encourage young men to become responsible risk takers. This is the kind of spirit that embraces individual excellence over group consciousness. This is the kind of spirit which concludes that "If You Believe It, You Can Achieve It."

In conclusion, "The Repair of the Human Spirit" is essential if we are ever to address the rapidly increasing educational concerns of young men that engulf public schools in America today. No amount of new technology, advanced degrees, professional development activities, sparkling new buildings, political involvement, curriculum enhancements, or business partnerships, can hope to replace the importance of repairing a child's "Wounded Spirit."

Far too long we have heard many young men described as lacking the spirit to win or having a defeated spirit or a young man having lost his spirit. If adults are to truly be thought of as good stewards in expanding the unlimited future of America, then we must insist on the immediate repair of the wounded spirits of many of our young men. We must reignite those flames of academic pride and self improvement in our young men that not too long ago appeared like roaring forest fires but, now appears to be smoky embers extinguishing itself at a very rapid pace.

We must renew in our young men a thirst for knowledge and to assure them that they have an expectation to utilize their immense intellectual talents at all times. We must resolve to empower our young men to define their own sense of purpose and to resist the notion of relying on total strangers to determine their true destiny. Young men must strive to become independent thinkers capable of mapping out comprehensive strategies when addressing complex issues. Young men as well as adults must recommit to becoming lifelong learners. How well we effectively weave together all of these divergent thoughts is essential if we are to systematically tackle the challenges confronting America's young men.

Money alone is not the answer! An overemphasis on new curriculum content minus relevancy and common sense will continue to be unproductive. The integration of positive, relevant student connections must be addressed. It will take a energized recommitment by well intentioned adults to earn the trust that is currently absent when discussing our relationship with young men. It is only then that we can say that the American Dream that has served as a beacon of hope for countless generations can once again be internalized as a realistic option by all 21st century young men.

ADVICE FOR MEANINGFUL 21ST CENTURY LIVING

1. Great achievements often involve great risk and even greater efforts.
2. When you lose, do not lose the lesson.
3. Follow the three Rs: Respect for self; Respect for others and; Responsibility for all your actions.
4. When you realize you have made a mistake, Huddle-Up and take immediate steps to correct it.
5. Be open to change but, do not ever lose your values.

President Barack Obama acknowledges that our country has entered into a period of new challenges and new responsibilities. A frontier that requires that each citizen share in the myriad of duties and assignments if we are to reach America's true potential! He concluded that there is nothing so satisfying to the spirit or the defining of one's character than giving our all to a very challenging task. We dare not fail! The fate of our young men will be decided by our collective resolve to succeed!

References

Cited:

Sheehy, Gail. Passages: Predictable Crises of Adult Life (1974), E.P. Dutton & Publishing Company Inc. New York, NY.

Sampson, Davis Dr, Jenkins, George Dr, and Hunt Rameck Dr. The Bond: Three Young Men Learn to Forgive and Reconnect with Their Fathers (2007). Riverhead Books a member of Penguin Group (USA), Inc. New York, NY.

Collins, Jim and Porras, Jerry I.: Built To Last: Successful Habits of Visionary Companies (2002). Harper Collins Publishers Inc. New York, NY.

Gurian, Michael. The Wonder of Boys: What Parents, Mentors and Educators Can Do To Shape Boys Into Exceptional Men (1996). Penguin Putnam Inc. New York, NY.

Johnson, Spencer, MD. Who Moved My Cheese? An A-Mazing Way to Deal with Change in Your Work and in Your Life (1998). G.P. Putnam's Sons Publishers. New York, NY.

Holliday, Henry E. Dr. Gender Education In 7 Steps: Reigniting the Academic Pilot Lights of Boys and Girls (2007). Instant Publisher. Atlanta, Ga.

Obama, Barack. The Audacity of Hope: Thoughts on Reclaiming The American Dream (2006). Crown Publishing Group, Division of Random House, New York, NY.

Fraser, George. Success Runs In Our Race (1994). Avon Books Publishing Company, New York, NY

Dobson, James, Dr. Bringing Up Boys: Practical Advice and Encouragement for those Shaping the Next Generation of Men (2001). Tyndale House Publishers, Inc. Wheaton, Illinois.

Cosby, Bill and Poussaint, Alvin F. Come On People: On the Path from Victims To Victors (2007). Thomas Nelson Publishing, Inc. Nashville, Tennessee.

Collins, Jim. Good To Great: Why Some Companies Make the Leap and Others Don't (2001). Harper Business an Imprint of Harper Collins Publishers, New York, NY.

Mathews, Jay. Class Struggles: What's Wrong (and Right) with America's Best Public High Schools (1998). Times Books Random House, New York, NY.

Peters, Stephen G. Do You Know Enough About Me To Teach Me? (2006). The Peters Group Foundation, Orangeburg, S.C.

Anyon, Jean. Ghetto Schooling: A Political Economy of Urban Educational Reform (1997). Teachers College Columbia University, New York, NY

Howard, Mike. From Ordinary to Extraordinary: Success Begins Within (2006). Instant Publisher, Atlanta, Georgia.

Clark, Reginald M. Family Life and School Achievement: Why Poor Black Children Succeed or Fail (1983). The University of Chicago Press, Chicago and London

Wynn, Mychal. Teaching, Parenting, and Mentoring Successful Black Males (2007). Rising Sun Publishing Company, Marietta, Georgia.

Sun, Tzu, Sunzi. The Art of War (1944), Military Service Publishing Company. As translated by Lionel Giles (2002). Dover Publications, Inc. Mineola, New, York.

Katz, Jackson, Ed. M. Tough Guise: Violence, Media and the Crisis in Masculinity (2002). Media Education Foundation, Northampton, Massachusetts.

Covey, Dr. Steven R. The 7 Habits of Highly Effective People (1989). Simon and Shuster, New York, New York.

Kunjufu, Dr. Jawanza. Countering the Conspiracy to Destroy Black Boys (1983), Afro-Am Publishing Co., Chicago, Illinois.

Gurian, Michael and Henley, Patricia. Boys and Girls Learn Differently: A Guide for Teachers and Parents (2001). Jossey-Bass, San Francisco, California.

Suttle, Earl, Dr. and Hubbard, John, Dr. Earl's Pearls On Enjoying Excellence, 30 Pearls of Wisdom (2003). Victory International Publishers, Atlanta, Georgia.

Jakes, T.D. Reposition Yourself: Living Life Without Limits (2007). A Division of Simon & Schuster, Inc. New York, NY.

Warren, Rick. The Purpose Driven Life: What On Earth Am I Here For? (2002). Zondervan Press, Grand Rapids, Michigan.

Kimbro, Dennis, Ph.D. What Makes the Great Great: Strategies for Extraordinary Achievement (1998). A Main Street Book Published by Bantam Doubleday Publishing Group, Inc. New York, NY.

Ziglar, Zig. Over the Top: Moving From Survival to Stability, From Stability to Success, From Success to Significance (1997). Thomas Nelson Publishers, Nashville, Tennessee.

Kindlon, Dan, and Thompson, Michael Ph.D. Raising Cain: Protecting the Emotional Life of Boys (1999). Ballantine Books, New York, NY.

Payne, Ruby K. A Framework for Understanding Poverty (2001). Aha! Process, Inc., Highlands, Texas.

Lezotte, Lawrence W. Correlates of Effective Schools: The First and Second Generation (1991) Effective Schools Products, Ltd., Okemos, Michigan.

Covey, Stephen M.R. The Speed of Trust: The One Thing That Changes Everything (2006). Free Press, A Division of Simon and Schuster, Inc. New York, NY.

Miller, Matt: The Tyranny of Dead Ideas: Letting Go of the Old Ways of Thinking to Unleash a New Prosperity (2009). Times Books Henry Holt and Company, L.L.C Publishers. New York, NY.

Other:

Gadsden, Vivian L. Transitions in Life Course of African-American Males: Issues In Schooling, Adulthood, Fatherhood, and Families (August 1995). University of Pennsylvania & William Trent University of Illinois. National Center on Fathers and Families.

Davis, Earl James, and Will Jordan, J. Determinants of School Success Among African American Males.

Anderson, Kerby. Loneliness (Aug19, 2008). Probe Ministries, Richardson, TX (1993). *http://wwwleaderu.com/orgs/probe/docs/lonely.html*

Smith, David. Men Without Friends, Six Barriers to Friendship pp. 5 *http://www.leaderu.com/orgs/probe/docs/lonely/html*

Oral Traditions Manual. What is an Oral Tradition? Northern Heritage Centre, Yellowknife, Northwest Territories, Canada (October 24, 2008). *http://pwnhc.learnnet.nt.ca/research/otm/otrman2.htm*

Schlosser, Eric. The Prison Industrial Complex. Atlantic Monthly, December. (1998). Pp. 51–77.

Harris, Maya. Prison vs. Education Spending Reveals California's Priorities (May 29, 2007).

Allen, Lili, Almeida, Cheryl, and Steinberg, Adria. From the Prison Track to the College Track: Pathways to Postsecondary Success for Out-of School Youth (May 16–17, 2003). In Jobs for the Future Prepared for School to Prison Pipeline.

Hestenes, Roberta, Dr. Crowded Loneliness. *http://www.leaderu.com/orgs/probe/docs/lonely.html*

Vitaro, Frank E, Tremblay, Richard E, Kerr, Margaret, Pagani, Linda, and Bukowski, William M. Disruptiveness, Friends' Characteristics and Delinquency in Early Adolescence: A Test of Two Competing Models of Development (August 1997). In Child Development, Vol. 68. No. 4. pages 676–689.

Newsweek. The Boy Crisis: At Every Level of Education They Are Falling Behind. What To Do? (January 30, 2006). New York, NY.

Kaplan, Leslie. Peer Pressure During Adolescence, Fall 1999. Developmental Psychology: Student Net Letter. Fall 1999. pp. 1–5. *www.mc.maricopa.edu/dept/d46/psy/dev/Fall99/peer_pres sure/index.html*

Shargel, Franklin Dr. Building America's Competitiveness: From the Schoolhouse to the Work place. Shargel Consulting, (2007) Albuquerque, New Mexico.

Barber, Benjamin R. How Markets Corrupt Children, Infantilize Adults, and Swallow Citizens Whole.

Byrne, Rhonda. The Secret: The Laws of Attraction, Obey Your Thoughts (2006). Atria books Beyond Words Publishing.

Ewers, James B. Jr. A Message from the Old School: Issues and Views (Spring 2008). The Crisis page 12.

Seneca, Anger and Violence: The greatest Remedy for Anger is delay.

Bawden, Terri. Teachers as Coaches. Wenatchee School District. October 24, 2008. pp. 1. *http://home.wsd.wednet.edu/WSD/Endrichment/teachercoach.html*

Teaching Boys: Teachers College Record Volume 110, Number 2, February 2008. pp. 443–481. Teachers College, Columbia University 0161–4681.

Singham, Mano. The Canary in the Mine: The Achievement Gap Between Black and White Students (September, 1998). Reproduced with permission of Phi Delta Kappan, pp. 9–15.

Swindoll, Charles. We Are In Charge of Our Attitudes. pp.132.

Brooks, Robert Ph.D. & Marx, Jeffrey. A Football Coach's Lessons for Life: To Nurture Respect and Dignity in Our Youth, Parade Magazine. *http://www. drrobertbrooks.com/writing/articles/0410.html*

Cardinal, Catherine, Ph.D. The Ten Commandments of Self Esteem (1998). Andrews McMeel Publishing, Kansas City, Missouri.

Re Branding: Perspectives on Corporate Branding Strategy 10 Steps to Successful Corporate Branding. Venture Republic 2002–2005.

Deutschman, Alan. Making Change or Die: What is it so darn hard to change our ways? Fast Company, (May 2005), San Francisco, California.

Simons, Janet A., Irwin, Donald B., and Drinnien, Beverly

A. Maslow's Hierarchy of Needs: The Search for Understanding. Psychology, 1987, West Publishing Company, New York, NY.

Fremon, Celeste & Hamilton, Stephaine Renfrow. Are schools failing black boys? Employment Law: Dawn D. Bennett-Alexander, Esq. Terry College of Business, University of Georgia. December 12, 2004.

Index

academic coaching, 98–99, 102
adolescent experience, 1
adult understanding of teenage language and slang, 17–18
advice for 21st-century living, 162
Alfange, Dean, Cornell University, 126–27
alienation, 21
alone, a poem, 26–26
American dream, 34
American middle class, 3
American nightmare, 34
angry boys, 84–85
at large community, 13, 31, 79
attitude, 123, 151
attitudinal survey, 33–34

boys and girls learning styles, 27, 107–108
branding, 34–35
Brown, James, singer songwriter, 31
buddy system, 74

census definition of family, 69
championship coaching for life, 153–56
change process, 42–45
character traits: an exercise, 53

characteristics model, 23
Choice, Charles Michael, poet:
    list of poems: "Individuality," 41–42; "Innocence of a Time Gone By," 69–70; "Of True Character," 124; "Tranquility Within," 128; "The Wind That Fills Our Sails," 131–32; "Stinging Words Causes Heart Pain," 157–58
chronically underperforming, 2
church attendance and GPA, 72
Clark, Reginald M., author, 74–76
coaches/coaching, 87, 92, 153–56
commandments: a list to live by, 47
coming of age period, 20
community elders, 70–71
comparison of athletic and academic practices, 95–98
core values, worth knowing, 5–6
corporate re-branding, 37–40
Covey, Steven, 57, 104, 156
crowded loneliness, 16–17

dash, the: analysis of the poem, 136
delayed gratification, 46–47
destiny: controlling it, 34, 39, 51
discipline, 66, 71, 85, 120–21

Index

Dromgoole, Will Allen, poet, 52

education and a nation's future, 2, 28–29
elders, 3–4, 70
effort/reward relationship, 77, 102
emotional bank account, 88
emotional branding, 40
emotional protection, 81

Fabre, Jean Henri, 19th-century French
    naturalist, 82–83
family, traditional/non-traditional, 69–76,
    87–89
first who...then what?, 67

gang membership, 76
Gaye, Marvin, 1; "Inner City Blues," 69;
    "What's Going On," 77
gender, 26–27, 108–12
gender-based classrooms, 113–14
Generation Y, 31–32
global economy, 1, 12
global society, 3, 13, 27, 33

Harold Melvin and the Blue Notes,
    71, 87
hierarchy theory of need, 6–8
hollywood version of manhood, 33–40
Howard, Mike, motivational speaker,
    47–48, 146. *See also* OPE (other
    peoples experience); OPK (other
    peoples knowledge); OPN (other
    peoples network)
huddle-up, 147

incarceration, 19, 23
industrial economy, 40
influential person, 52–53
intangibles of life, 148–51
intelligence quotient, (IQ), 91–92
interconnectedness, 13
intergenerational, 13
isolation, 13, 81. *See also* loneliness; male
    loneliness

Jackson, Michael, pop singer, 131;
    Analysis of the song "Man In the
    Mirror," 131

keep the end in mind, 156
Kennesaw State University, Kennesaw,
    GA, 84

"Lean On Me," a song, 51. *See also*
    Withers, Bill
Life-long learners, 126, 129
loneliness, 13–14. *See also* isolation; male
    loneliness

male defiance, 81–82
male leadership conference:
    example of developing of, 58–65
male loneliness, 14–16. *See also*
    loneliness
masculinity, 40–41
Maslow, Abraham, 6–8.
    See also hierarchy theory of needs
mean moms, a poem, 77–78
mentoring programs, 51–58
metaphors, definition, 93–94
micro inequities, 115
microwave generation, 31
Million Dollar Roundtable Organization,
    Cornell University, 126
Minority Student Retention Program
    (AAMI), Kennesaw State University,
    GA, 64
modern branding, two types, 40

NCLB (No Child Left Behind), 104
national brands, 39–40
national security and education, 41
nature vs. nurture, 90–92
networking good habits, 57–58
new and old ways of thinking, 48–49
new global economy, 40
new value system, 1, 104
non-verbal communication, 89,
    103–107

OPE (other peoples experience), 47.
  See also Howard, Mike
OPK (other people's knowledge), 47.
  See also Howard, Mike
OPN (other people's network), 47.
  See also Howard, Mike
observation of young males, 26–27, 29
opportunityisnowhere, what is this, 48.
  See also Howard, Mike
oppositional aggressive hyperactivity, 25
oral traditions, 2–3, 104, 150

packaging your brand, 36
paradigm pioneers, 133, 134
peers and peer pressure, 24–25, 81
peer groups, 25
peer influence model, 24–25
Pendergrass, Teddy, 87.
  See also Harold Melvin and the
    Blue Notes
personal brands, 34–7
personal value, 92
President Barack Obama, 39, 123, 162
prison industrial complex, 19–21

R. Kelly, singer, poet: an analysis of a
    song, "I believe I Can Fly," 145
rebranding, 34–50
redefining males, 34, 46, 50
reconnect, 85
repositioning, 127–28

sage on a stage, 101
sagging pants, 72
scholar athletes, 94, 97
Schott Foundation for Education, 21
self esteem, 4, 47, 55
self fulfilling prophecy, 19, 92
self introspection, 50
self motivation, 142
seven traits of change readiness, 43–44
Sly and The Family Stone, musical
    artist: "You Can Make It If You
    Try," 123

society's value, 20
special education student (SPED), 117–20
status quo, 110, 128
starfish story, 132–33;
  an analysis of the story, 133
stakeholders, 33–34, 37–38
structural changes, 25 years of, 10–13
student achievement pyramid of inter-
    vention 117–18
successful schools, 90
Sun Tzu, *The Art of War*, 129–30

Tabula Rasa Thesis, 90–91
teachers as coaches, 98–102
teaching strategies, 114–15
testosterone impact, 9–10
the bridge builder, a poem, 52.
  See also Dromgoole, Will Allen
the cheese has moved, 49–50
the company you keep, a poem, 67
things I have learned about young men,
    159–60
third grade failure syndrome, 19–24
three legged stool (triad), 148
three pillars of a good brand, 35

Title IX, 109–10
toxic people, 46
toxic relationship, 69, 115
traditional knowledge, 3–4
transitioning after high school, 21–23
trust, 142–43
Tubbs, Dr. J. Eric, college professor, 62
Tupac, Shakur, 15, 18–19:
  list of poems: "Sometimes I Cry," 15;
    "In the Depths of Solitude Dedicated
    2 Me," 18
twenty-first century skill sets, 43–44

urban center's high schools, 21

values, 37, 136
verbal and non-verbal cues, 103, 107
vision, 23, 27, 37, 131–35

wake up everybody, 87.
  See also Pendergrass, Teddy
what boys need, 79, 81
what really makes a difference, 66
winners and losers a poem, 140
  author unknown
Withers, Bill, 51.
  See also "Lean on Me"
women and male disconnect, 83–84
wounded human spirit, 158
www.edtransform.com, 33, 105

X, Malcolm, 79–80
Xavier University, New Orleans, LA: Freshmen
  Curriculum, 101

Zeitgeist, the definition, 90–91
zero tolerance, 20
Ziglar, Zig, author and motivational
  speaker, 45, 47

About the Author

Dr. H. E. Holliday has been a school principal for parts of four different decades (1970–2005) in Ohio and Georgia at the middle-and high-school levels. His schools have long been recognized for exceeding academic expectations because of his willingness to take acceptable risk, his sensible and savvy leadership talents, and his success as a change agent.

He earned his PhD in educational leadership from The Ohio State University, where he was selected by his professors as the top scholar in his class. Doc Holliday has served as a classroom teacher (rural) and as principal of both middle and high schools. He has been an assistant superintendent for school improvement for the Cobb County, Georgia, Public School District (suburban), as well as chief of staff for the Atlanta Public Schools (urban).

He is a leader in developing innovative, data-driven programs for high-risk, under-performing schools with diverse populations. One of his most important contributions to public education is having produced over 50 educators who have gone on to become successful principals and university leaders across the United States.

He believes that public schools must learn how to take advantage of uncharted opportunities and how to stretch the few assets within their control. It is just like anything else: We must learn to do more with less! Dr. Holliday is also a sought-after lecturer and presenter because of his wealth of knowledge in the field of education over the past 30 years. He has presented at state, regional, national and international conferences across the United States.

Doc Holliday is currently associate professor at Kennesaw State University (Georgia). He has been married to Sarah for 34 years and has two children, Monica and Joshua.